BY UNDERGROUND TO THE ZOO

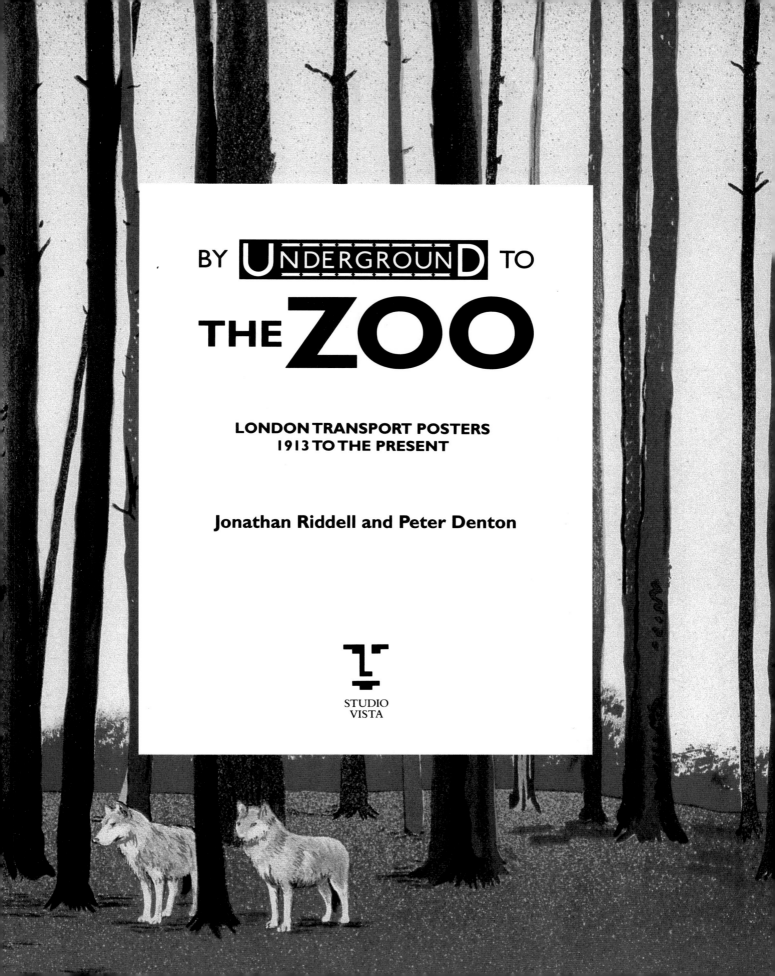

BY UNDERGROUND TO
THE ZOO

LONDON TRANSPORT POSTERS
1913 TO THE PRESENT

Jonathan Riddell and Peter Denton

STUDIO
VISTA

ACKNOWLEDGEMENTS

With the exception of the London County Council
Tramways' posters on pages 24, 31 (right), 41 (right),
43, 51, 52, 53 (above), 56, 58 (right), 60 (left) and
62 (left), which have been reproduced by kind
permission of the Corporation of London, Greater
London Record Office, all the posters in this book are
reproduced from the London Transport Museum's
poster collection. The crest on page 12 is © Zoological
Society of London and is reproduced with their kind
permission.

STUDIO VISTA

A Cassell Imprint
Wellington House
125 Strand
London WC2R 0BB

Copyright © London Transport Museum 1995
We're All Going to the Zoo copyright © The Zoological Society of London 1995
First published 1995

British Library Cataloguing in Publication Data
A catalogue record for this book is available from the British Library

ISBN 0-289-80133-8

Typeset by Litho Link Ltd, Welshpool, Powys, Wales
Printed and bound in Great Britain by Bath Colour Books Ltd

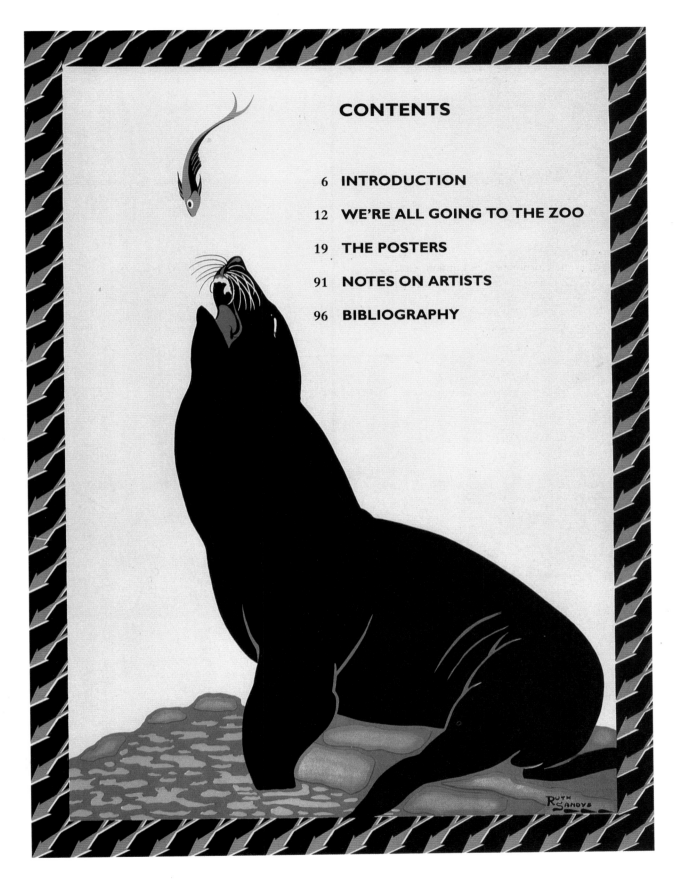

CONTENTS

INTRODUCTION

CAMDEN TOWN is the nearest Underground Station, being within a few minutes' walk of the Zoo. Regent's Park is also convenient, as Motor-buses run therefrom to within a short distance of the main entrance of the Gardens, which may also be reached by a pleasant walk across the Park from this station.

Motor-bus No 74, which connects with Warwick Avenue and Camden Town Underground Stations, passes the Zoo, and the routes of many other services are adjacent.

 his quotation comes from a small booklet about London Zoo which was published by the Underground in 1915. Some distance from any other major tourist attraction in central London, the Zoo was probably the most inaccessible by Underground: to get there meant a brisk walk or bus ride from Camden Town, Chalk Farm, Regent's Park, St John's Wood or Baker Street stations. All these have been advertised on posters as being convenient for the Zoo. All are certainly about the same distance from the Zoo, yet none is close enough, if judged by the exacting expectations of Londoners who expect most central venues to be directly outside an Underground station. Of course, each of these named stations has its merits for getting to the Zoo, depending upon where you are travelling from; yet a glance at the posters in this book suggests that neither the Underground nor, later, London Transport could make up its mind about which particular station it should promote.

It was in 1908, just two years after the formation of the Underground Group of Companies, that Frank Pick, in charge of publicity and officially assistant to the General Manager, issued the Underground's first pictorial posters. Eleven were produced in that year, but it was not until five years later, in 1913, that the first one advertising London Zoo appeared. It was not clear why it took so long before a Zoo poster was issued, as it must surely have offered a fascinating choice of colourful subjects. Unfortunately the First World War soon followed and, although posters advertising the Underground still appeared, it was not for another three years that the next poster promoting the Zoo was seen. After the war the Zoo became a favourite subject for the

LONDON CHARACTERS · E·A·COX·

THE ZOO KEEPER — BOOK TO — REGENTS PARK OR CAMDEN TOWN — FOR THE ZOO —

Underground's posters and, along with Kew Gardens and Hampton Court, was soon one of the most popular locations to feature on them. The animals always provided the main inspiration behind each poster, with perhaps the exception of E A Cox's 'The Zoo Keeper' (page 25), where the human element took precedence. The choice of animal and style was often left to the artist but sometimes a major event, such as the opening of the aquarium in 1924, may have been specified by the Underground's Publicity Officer.

In common with that of many other transport undertakings, the early public image and financial performance of London's underground railways was not good. But in 1907 Albert Stanley was appointed General Manager, and as a result there was a dramatic improvement in the fortunes of the company. However, Stanley (later Lord Ashfield) cannot claim all the responsibility for this turnaround, for when Frank Pick joined the company in 1906 he was so critical of its publicity that Stanley suggested he should take over responsibility for it. Pick, who had qualified as a solicitor, had no previous experience of advertising but this did not deter him. Before moving to the Underground he had worked as personal assistant to the North Eastern Railway's General Manager, Sir George Gibb, who had himself transferred to the Underground a couple of years before, and it is highly probable that Pick had been influenced by the North Eastern's publicity which at the time was among the best of all the railway companies'.

The Underground had not been planned as a unified network but was originally built as a series of independent lines, each to be operated independently. Although it was not long before most of these lines came under the control of the Underground Group, each line still retained much of its own identity. Pick saw the necessity of creating a strong corporate image which would suggest to Londoners that the Underground was a coherent system allowing travellers to reach all parts of the capital.

Although the Underground was not the first railway company to use posters for publicity purposes, it very quickly became one of the most successful. From the start the image portrayed was that everywhere in London was accessible by the company's Underground trains, and later by its buses and trams. Naturally no mention was made of the fact that some locations, including the Zoo, were also served by trains other than the Underground's. The Metropolitan Railway, the world's first underground railway, opened between Paddington and Farringdon in 1863. It remained an independent company until 1933, and its service to Baker Street Station would have been just as convenient for the Zoo as was the Underground's service to Regent's Park or Camden Town stations – depending, of course, upon the direction from which one was travelling.

During the years leading up to the First World War the motorbus finally triumphed over the horsebus. When the Underground Group took over the capital's buses in 1913 Frank Pick was keen to promote the benefits of this new mode of travel, and in particular to encourage leisure travel to the country on Sundays. One would, therefore, also have expected many of the posters promoting travel to the Zoo to recommend the company's newly acquired bus services. But they did not, even though route 49 from Camden Town to Clapham Junction, which passed within 200 yards of the Zoo's main entrance, had started by September 1912, replacing an earlier and short-lived service on route 33. This new service was, however, also to be short-lived, and in December 1912 that particular section of the route was taken over by the 74, which ran from Camden Town Station to Kensington Gardens. It is surprising that the Underground apparently felt no need to promote its bus services to the Zoo, especially since they were much more direct than the Underground's own trains. Even today, more passengers travel away from the Zoo by bus than arrive there on a bus, and apart from a colourful leaflet issued by London Northern (page 96) there have been few attempts to encourage visitors to the Zoo to arrive by bus.

Pick was concerned not just with the image and message on individual posters but also with the presentation of the whole Underground system; this included the siting and display of posters. Before he took the matter in hand they had been displayed in a jumbled mass with little if any thought as to how they would be seen. So Pick selected special sites which would exhibit only the company's own posters, to help promote a clear corporate message which would not get lost amongst the general mass of advertising material. Pick believed that by providing clear information about services, and the latest improvements to the system, passengers would soon feel themselves to be a part of the system and want to use it more.

Posters were not the only medium used. A wide variety of publicity material such as regular press advertisements and occasional booklets, including the one on the Zoo which was published in 1915, soon appeared. In order to enhance the corporate image further he commissioned the typographer Edward Johnston to design a typeface for the exclusive use of the company. This sans-serif face first appeared in 1916 and, along with Eric Gill's new typeface Gill Sans, set new standards and was far ahead of its time. It was originally designed for station signs but soon began to be used on posters. It is still used today by London Transport, although in a modified form to suit computer technology.

The very first pictorial posters were usually commissioned from printers, such as Waterlow and Son, and Johnson Riddle, who employed their own commercial artists. Little, if anything, is known about most of these studio artists; the quality of their work was varied, but at its best could rival that of any fine artists of the time. Pick, however, felt that he could achieve better results by commissioning work directly from the artist, and sometimes an artist would approach him in the hope of obtaining a commission. One reason for the success of Pick's commissions lies in the artists used, who reflected a broad range of tastes and styles. Even Pick could not hope that every poster would be successful, but the quantity commissioned allowed room for the occasional failure. Posters were designed not just to appear on station walls, bus shelters and hoardings but also on and in the company's buses, trams and Underground trains.

It was not long before the Underground, and Pick himself, gained a high reputation for the quality of the Group's advertising and design. He did not limit his commissions to commercial artists but also approached fine artists, who in the early years were not keen to venture into the advertising field because they felt that such work was beneath them. Contacts with the noted artist and lithographer Ernest Jackson soon led to a series of lithographs by members of the Senefelder Club, a society for the encouragement of autolithography (and named after the inventor of lithography, Alois Senefelder). Fortunately for Pick, technological changes at this time were working to his advantage, notably the increasing use of the offset printing machine, which no longer required a mirror image of the artist's design to be drawn on a stone or metal plate.

Pick did not follow fashion, but set it, and was not afraid to commission work from unknown artists. In 1915, for instance, Pick was the first to commission the American Edward McKnight Kauffer, who was to become one of Britain's most noted poster designers. As a result of this adventurous policy the Underground gained a reputation as one of the country's foremost art patrons. In the two decades between the wars a new poster by McKnight Kauffer was an eagerly awaited event, although unfortunately he never designed one to advertise the Zoo. Today, as in 1908, only a few pictorial posters are produced, but in the 1920s and 1930s the poster was probably the most important form of advertising for the Underground, with up to 60 pictorial posters produced each year.

The year 1933 saw the formation of the London Passenger Transport Board. It replaced the Underground Group of Companies and also included the Metropolitan Railway and the London County Council Tramways, many of whose posters are reproduced in this book, as well as several other small operators. Both the Metropolitan Railway and London County Council Tramways produced their own distinctive, and sometimes very high-quality, posters, but not on a scale to compare with those of the Underground. Although the Metropolitan Railway advertised travel to the Thames, and to the countryside for rambles, fishing or golf, the London Transport Museum does not contain a single pictorial poster encouraging the Metropolitan's passengers to travel to the Zoo.

The Second World War had an immediate effect on all aspects of London Transport. The company's buses were not requisitioned to take troops to the front as they had been during the First World War, but rationing, the claims of the war effort and for the first time large-scale destruction from bombing meant that London Transport was affected to a much greater extent than before. Pictorial poster production ceased almost completely: the few that were produced were propaganda for the war

UNDERGROUND

OFF TO THE ZOO

BOOK TO
REGENTS PARK OR
CAMDEN TOWN

effort. Frank Pick resigned from London Transport in 1940. McKnight Kauffer, as an American, was a neutral alien and decided he was not wanted in England. The departure of these two men inevitably had a disastrous effect on the production of posters for London Transport. Although the Zoo closed only for a short while in 1939, between 1939 and 1948 no posters promoting the Zoo were produced, contrasting with the two that came out during the First World War (above and pages 21 and 22 (left)).

Shortly after the end of the war the London Passenger Transport Board, soon to become the nationalised London Transport Executive, a part of the newly formed British Transport Commission, decided to try to regain its lead in the poster field. A new publicity officer, Harold F Hutchison, was appointed in 1947. Hutchison had spent several years in advertising, and was well aware of the high standards which Pick had set. It was a hard act to follow. At first the emphasis of the message was changed. Suffering from the depredations of the war years, London Transport felt it should explain to its passengers the problems involved in operating the world's largest urban passenger system rather than continue the pre-war message of encouraging travel. To some extent this message was not entirely new. Attempts had frequently been made through posters and other publicity to explain the difficulties of operating what was then a new form of travel.

Although the output under Hutchison could never compare with that of Pick, he did play an important role in the history of the London Transport poster. He invented, or perhaps rather developed, the idea of the pair poster, in which two double royal size posters were displayed together; one half was devoted entirely to text, with perhaps a decorative border, while on the other the artist could have a free hand. Examples of this type of poster appear on pages 78 and 80, along with the more traditional landscape quad-royal format on page 50 (below). But although Hutchison commissioned several exciting new designers and artists, such as Hans Unger (pages 80 (right) and 84–5), John Burningham (page 84 (left)), William Roberts (page 79) and David Gentleman, the total number of commissions was falling.

In the mid-1960s Bryce Beaumont replaced Hutchison as Publicity Officer. He had joined London Transport in the 1930s as a copywriter and had a detailed knowledge of London Transport's posters, but this did not prevent the pictorial poster programme from continuing its rapid decline, By the time Michael Levey took over in 1975 the number of posters directly commissioned from artists had dropped to as few as four a year. There was no single reason for this decline, but it was clear that pictorial posters now formed only a minor part of the new marketing strategy: London Transport increasingly used both radio and television to advertise its services. The appointment in 1970 of Foote Cone and Belding as London Transport's first advertising agency could not have helped, as it led to a further loss of direct contact with the artist. Occasionally memorable images were produced, such as Abram Games' classic poster of 1976 'London Zoo' (page 89), which was a direct commission. This is not to say that FCB did not produce work of a high quality. Sometimes they did, but it was in neither the same tradition nor the same style as the classic Underground posters of the past.

In 1984 London Transport became London Regional Transport, with two subsidiary companies, London Underground Ltd and London Buses Ltd. At the time this change may have seemed cosmetic to its many passengers, but it set the stage for the eventual break-up of the system which for the last 50 years had been operated by one company. Surprisingly, rather than sounding the death knell for the London Transport poster, this may have directly led to a new style of poster and a stay of execution.

In 1986 London Underground Ltd, under their Marketing Director, Dr Henry Fitzhugh, renewed the policy of commissioning art posters. Fitzhugh, who was an aeronautical engineer by profession and had been in charge of London Transport's scientific laboratories, had no previous experience of commissioning artists. In this respect he was like Frank Pick. To begin with he commissioned an agent to find suitable artists, but as his knowledge grew he quickly began to go directly to artists. These latest pictorial posters soon became a separate series, and were given the name 'Art On The Underground', now forming a distinctive set of commissions separate from other publicity on the Underground. A wide range of styles has been achieved, constrained only by the comparatively small number of commissions of no more than four or six posters a year. Fitzhugh chose both graphic designers and fine artists, but perhaps more of the latter. The original aim of these posters was to act as fillers during a period of decline in commercial advertising on the Underground, and to be appreciated as art. To date there have been over 50 of these posters; although some subjects, such as the Royal Academy, have appeared more than once, there has been only one poster for the Zoo. The programme has now been taken over by London Transport's Design Director, Jeremy Rewse-Davies, who hopes to commission more graphic designers than did Fitzhugh.

GREEN LINE TO WHIPSNADE

In 1931 the Zoological Society opened Whipsnade to complement the collection housed in London. Just outside Dunstable in rural Bedfordshire, it was set in over 600 acres and allowed the public to view some of the Zoo's animals in a rural and perhaps more realistic setting than the confined spaces at Regent's Park. In the 1930s London Transport served a much wider area than today. Its Green Line coach routes, which began in 1930, together with its Country Bus network, extended far out into the home counties – as far afield as Guildford and East Grinstead in the south and Bishops Stortford and Dunstable in the north. London Transport saw in Whipsnade an ideal attraction to which, in season at least, it could convey large numbers of passengers with as yet little competition from the motor car. What was more, nearly all the journeys would be return trips (at London Zoo, if you recall, fewer people arrived by bus than left by bus). Return tickets were available for only 4s / 6d (22½p), either by through coach or via the London Midland and Scottish Railway's service from St Pancras Station to St Albans City Station, as it was then known, where passengers could transfer to London Transport's Country Bus route 368.

Posters such as that by Anrid Johnston in 1932 (page 60 (right) portrayed a rather idealised scene: wolves and deer, bears and zebras would never be allowed to mix, although they did have the freedom of large paddocks. Michael Ross's 1936 poster (page 72) gives a much truer picture of the wolves – one that has hardly changed today, as Whipsnade now has the largest pack of European wolves in England. In the late 1940s posters and leaflets advertised 'A Sunday Excursion by London Transport Coach'. But with the post-war growth of private motoring the role of the Green Line coaches and Country Buses declined. More people travelled by car to Whipsnade. In 1970, when control of London Transport was passed to the Greater London Council, Green Line coaches and Country Buses were transferred to the National Bus Company. But long before this time there had been a great decline in the number of posters depicting Whipsnade. This was partly a result in the decline of the poster in general as an advertising medium for London Transport, but also a reflection of changing travel patterns.

LONDON COUNTY COUNCIL TRAMWAYS

Before 1933 the Underground was not the only provider of public transport in central London. In addition to the trams operated by the Underground Group, London County Council had its own extensive system of tram routes which complemented those belonging to the Underground. Like the Underground, none of the LCC's routes directly served the Zoo; but nine routes did serve Camden Town, and during the 1920s and 1930s the CCT pictorial posters directed passengers there. By 1910 London County Council Tramways was the largest tram operator in the country. Its programme of pictorial posters began in the early 1920s and soon developed its own house style. Posters were issued right up until its takeover by the London Passenger Transport Board in 1933, when all of London's tramways were combined for the first time.

In February 1922 the London County Council's Central School of Arts and Crafts reached an agreement with London County Council Tramways, by which its students would design posters to be displayed on trams. First to appear was a series of 12 posters in two different formats from those of the Underground. The smaller size

would appear on the end panels inside the saloons of the tramcars as well as on the outside, while the much larger four-sheet posters were intended to be displayed on the large tramway shelters which had been erected at busy points on the network. Often the same design was adapted to suit both formats. The total number of poster designs issued is not known but certainly exceeded 160 – compared to over 3,000 produced by London Transport. But, of course, it must be remembered that London Transport is still producing posters more than 60 years after the demise of the London County Council Tramways as a separate concern. It is a shame that the posters of the LCC Tramways are not better known.

This book has brought together for the first time most of London Transport and London County Council posters advertising London and Whipsnade Zoos. The concentration on 1920s' and 1930s' posters is an accurate reflection of the larger numbers issued in those years. With one or two exceptions, none of these posters was part of a larger series, or of a campaign advertising a range of destinations, as was the case with many posters included in the earlier book *By Underground to Kew*.

PRINTING

The skill of the printer was second only in importance to the skill of the artist. The printing of mass-produced posters depended on the technology available at the time. By 1908, when London Transport's first pictorial poster appeared, lithography had already become well established. As a result, most of London Transport's posters were produced using the commercial lithographic process, in which the artist's original design was redrawn by a lithographer in the printer's workshop. This process depended on highly skilled craftsmen, whose job was to redraw the artist's design. Often the lithographer had to adapt the artist's work to accommodate the limitations of the printing process.

Originally lithography involved converting the artist's design into a mirror image, which would then be printed on to the paper, but by 1910 offset lithography was introduced. This removed the need for a reversed image to be drawn manually, as the machine could now reverse the image itself. A further development in the 1950s resulted in the role of the skilled lithographer being superseded by photolithography, in which the artist's design was copied photographically on to a plate.

A small number of the Underground's posters were drawn directly on to the stone by the artist himself, bypassing the role of the lithographer. This is known as autolithography. Most commercial artists, however, preferred to leave this stage to the printer.

SIZES

Most of the posters illustrated in this book were originally issued in the double royal size (40 × 25in/101.6 × 63.5cm). These posters normally appeared on and outside Underground stations, and this was the standard size for both Underground and main line railways. Less common was the double crown (30 × 20in /76.2 × 50.8cm), which originally appeared on the fronts of buses and the side panels of trams, and occasionally in stations. Today this size is used for some of the posters in the 'Art on the Underground' series. These two sizes formed the basis for other sizes, such as quad royal (40 × 50in/101.6 × 127cm), four sheet (40 × 60in/101.6 × 152.4cm), and the much larger trackside posters which were rarely used for the company's own pictorial posters. The four sheet poster was not very common and was originally used in the landscape (horizontal) format, except by London County Council Tramways where it appeared in a portrait (vertical) format. Today the four sheet has achieved widespread use on the Underground in portrait format as the standard size for the 'Art on the Underground' series. The small panel posters were produced in a variety of sizes to fit advertising spaces inside buses and Underground trains and also on bus stops. No single standard size was employed, but rather a multitude of sizes to fit the particular locations for which they were intended.

SELECTIVE CHRONOLOGY

The posters reproduced here are primarily advertisements, and could only promote the services which the Underground was able to provide at the time they were commissioned. The following chronology is an attempt to list the major developments in the growth of the Underground, later London Transport, in relation to the posters. Other developments which, although important in themselves, do not impinge on the subject of the book, have been omitted.

1863 Opening of the Metropolitan Railway between Paddington and Farringdon, the world's first underground railway.

1871 Camden Town and Bayswater Association operated the first horsebus service past the Zoo.

1902 Incorporation of the Underground Electric Railway Company (Underground Group), which originally comprised the District Railway and the projected Bakerloo, Piccadilly and Hampstead tube lines.

1906 Baker Street and Waterloo (Bakerloo) Railway opened.

1907 Charing Cross, Euston and Hampstead Railway (Northern Line) opened.

1908 First pictorial poster issued by the Underground.

1910 First reliable mass-produced motorbus (B Type) introduced by the London General Omnibus Company (LGOC).

1911 First motorbus service to the Zoo (Route 33) was operated by the LGOC from 11 January.

1912 The Underground Group took control of the LGOC, which by 1914 had a virtual monopoly of London's buses.

1913 The Central London Railway (Central Line) and the City and South London Railway (City branch of the Northern Line) were taken over by the Underground Group.

1913 First pictorial poster for the Zoo issued by the Underground.

1930 Green Line coaches started.

1931 Whipsnade Zoo opened.

1933 London Passenger Transport Board (LPTB) formed, with powers to take over and operate all bus, tram, trolleybus and Underground services in London.

1947 LPTB nationalised and renamed the London Transport Executive.

1970 Green Line coaches and Country Buses transferred to London Country Bus Services Ltd, a subsidiary of the National Bus Company.

1984 London Regional Transport created.

1985 Two subsidiary companies, London Buses Ltd and London Underground Ltd, were formed to run bus and Underground services.

1994 London Regional Transport required to sell off its bus companies.

WE'RE ALL GOING TO THE ZOO

PETER DENTON

The London Zoo has been regarded by the public for many years as a national exhibition along with such places as the Tower, the British Museum and Kew Gardens. Few of the public will admit to not having been to the Zoo, yet few are aware that this great collection has been built up, maintained and financed by a private society.

Consultant's report, January 1970

A QUEST FOR KNOWLEDGE

ondon Zoo, occupying 36 acres in Regent's Park, is regarded by many as the oldest and most prestigious zoological institution in the world. Alas, neither statement is true. The Jardin des Plantes in Paris dates from 1794, and many other zoos now enjoy regular public funding to capitalise on man's enduring love of animals. London Zoo does, however, retain a unique and enviable quality. It is part of the Zoological Society of London, the world's first zoological society, whose driving force was the quest for knowledge. For this enlightened approach we must thank Sir Humphry Davy (1778–1829), President of the Royal Society and the inventor of the miners' safety lamp which bears his name. Davy's chief partner in founding the Zoological Society was Sir Stamford Raffles (1781–1826), explorer, merchant, anti-slave trade campaigner, founder of Singapore and a man of high intellect. Towards the end of his life, he recalled visiting the Paris Zoological Garden in 1817. On his final return home he set about establishing the British equivalent.

In 1825 Davy, Raffles and others published a prospectus for the establishment of a society to study zoology. Premises were obtained in Bruton Street, and then on 29 April 1826 the Zoological Society of London was founded with Raffles as President. He officiated at just one Council meeting before dying of a brain tumour on 5 July 1826, the day before his forty-fifth birthday.

In 1829 the new Society was granted a royal charter by King William IV 'for the advancement of Zoology and animal physiology and the introduction of new and curious subjects of the animal kingdom'. It may have been quaint phraseology, but it emphasised the Society's scientific origins. A farm was bought that year at Kingston in Surrey to allow animals to be reared in a more rural atmosphere than that of London. This forerunner of Whipsnade lasted only five years, however, before being closed on grounds of cost. A museum was started in the Bruton Street premises, stocked partly by Charles Darwin, who collected many unusual species specifically for the museum during his famous voyage on the *Beagle*. The exhibits formed the basis for what is now the British Museum of Natural History when the Society sold them in 1855. The Zoological Society's library dates from the earliest meetings and is actually older than the Zoo: it remains one of the world's leading zoological libraries. Further initiatives of the infant Society included the holding of scientific meetings and the regular publication of learned papers.

A GROWING COLLECTION

Five acres in the Regent's Park were leased to the Society by 'The Commissioners of Woods and Forests', and the Zoological Gardens were opened to the Fellows of the Society in 1828. The eminent Decimus Burton (1800–81) was appointed architect to the Society in 1830. Most of his buildings were designed in a style that owed much to John Nash, originator of the Regent's Park. Much of Burton's work remains. The Ravens' Cage, the Zoo's oldest surviving structure, is listed Grade II and visible in the Members' Lawn, while the Clock Tower (adjacent to the Ravens' Cage) and the East Tunnel, which gives access to the Middle Gardens without having to cross the Outer Circle, are still in everyday use. Burton's Camel House in the Middle Gardens dates from 1837 – perhaps no other zoological building has housed for so long the same species for which it was built. Other early Zoo buildings, designed more for practical considerations than to achieve architectural grandeur, tried to reflect the environment and customs of the countries where their occupants originated: grass-thatched huts for the African antelopes, Swiss chalets for the goats, and British agricultural styles for domestic stock. But none of these buildings now remains. Anthony Salvin, Jnr was the most notable of the

Victorian architects. The African Aviary of 1990 incorporates his earlier Eastern Aviary, while the former Refreshment Rooms, later the Parrot House and soon to metamorphose as the Invertebrate Centre, owes much to Salvin's cottage *orné* influence. Buildings designed by Salvin but since demolished included a Monkey House (1864) and an Elephant and Rhino House (1868). His Lion House (1875) survived to 1974.

GOING PUBLIC

For the first twenty years of its existence, patronage of the Zoological Gardens had been restricted to elected Fellows of the Society and their guests. But in 1847 a financial crisis hit the Society, and to boost income the public were allowed into the Gardens on payment of 1s (5p), which remained the admission charge until 1942. The improved trading position enabled the Society to establish itself as a centre of excellence, assisted no doubt by a genuine enthusiasm amongst the *cognoscenti* to capitalise on the golden age of exploration and to see for themselves the fruits of the intrepid travellers. Throughout the mid-Victorian period the Gardens slowly increased in size to accommodate an ever-increasing number of species. The early buildings included the world's first Reptile House, dating from 1849, while the Fish House, the first-ever public marine aquarium, was opened in 1853. An Insect House, again a 'first', was opened in 1881. By 1867 the Zoological Gardens had become firmly established as a fashionable place to be seen. The music hall artist known as 'The Great Vance' popularised them with a song entitled 'Walking in the Zoo on Sunday'. This was the first time that the word 'Zoo' had appeared as a corruption of 'Zoological'.

> The Stilton, Sir, the cheese, the OK thing to do
> On Sunday afternoon is to toddle in the Zoo.

Influential figures in the Society in the mid- to late 19th century included Abraham Bartlett, Superintendent of the Gardens from 1859 to 1897. Officers of the Society included Philip Sclater, who was Secretary from 1859 to 1903, while the Prince Consort was President from 1851 until his untimely death in 1862. Four generations of the Drummond banking family were Treasurers between 1831 and 1945. The Society still banks with the successors to Drummonds, the Royal Bank of Scotland.

A BREATH OF FRESH AIR

The appointment in 1903 of the young zoologist Peter Chalmers Mitchell as Secretary of the Society heralded a renaissance in building at the Zoo. Chalmers Mitchell believed that fresh air was good for animals, even those native to tropical climates; he also had been quite impressed by the Hamburg Zoological Garden's use of electric lighting. Previously, most of the London Zoo animals had been kept in over-heated and badly lit accommodation, a haven for the spread of disease.

Although he was a scientist with little real commercial expertise, Chalmers Mitchell embarked almost single-handedly on an ambitious development plan featuring a Sea Lion Pond (1905), the Society's first attempt to introduce a naturalistic element to the display: penguins lived alongside the sealions. A far more ambitious scheme that developed from this scheme was the Mappin Terraces, a series of artificial mountains whose lower slopes housed all kinds of aquatic mammals and birds. The Terraces were named after Sir John Newton Mappin, a manufacturing silversmith who donated £20,000. Now listed Grade II, they represent one of the earliest known uses of pre-stressed concrete. Visitors were perhaps more impressed by the fact that the Terraces provided clear, uninterrupted viewing and, later, a café.

Much of the area under the Terraces is occupied by the Aquarium which, when opened in 1924, was one of the largest and most ambitious in the world. Although over the years various schemes have been considered to redevelop the Aquarium, it remains today much as when it was first built, although the complex electrical, oxygen, steam and water services have been upgraded to satisfy the Health and Safety Inspectors and to take advantage of modern technology, particularly with regard to energy conservation.

The architect John James Joass (1868–1952), who had been brought in by Chalmers Mitchell, was responsible for building the Society's offices in Regent's Park (1910). The old offices in Hanover Square, bought in 1843 when the Bruton Street premises proved inadequate, were then sold, and the proceeds helped to meet the costs of the Aquarium. Joass also designed the Regent Building (1929), containing the Zoo cafeteria and the Fellows' Restaurant, and the Pavilion Building (1921), now a shop. Sir Guy Dawber (1862–1938), President of the Royal Institution of British Architects in 1925–7, was his successor; his Reptile House of 1927 and Main Gate of 1928 owe much to the 'house style' set by Joass.

The Gorilla House of 1932 represented a major break with tradition. A young architect of Russian origin, Berthold Lubetkin (1901–90), was commissioned to design a building which perpetuated the fresh air theme whilst providing adequate winter housing, all the time allowing the public uninterrupted viewing. A Grade I listed building, the Gorilla House, shortly to be recommissioned as the Madagascar Centre, is loved by a few and hated by many, and it certainly caused a sensation when it was built. Of stark, concrete construction, it broke the Zoo's architectural mould and remains an enigma amongst the other buildings, which are mostly traditional. But Lubetkin impressed the authorities enough to be asked to design the Penguin Pool (1934), another Grade I listed building. An altogether more elegant structure, it remains a firm favourite with Zoo visitors, as much for the antics of its occupants, the Humboldt penguins, as for the photogenic qualities of its architecture.

THE ZOO IN THE COUNTRY

The Whipsnade estate, occupying some 600 acres of the Chiltern Hills in Bedfordshire, was purchased by the Society in 1927. Referred to by Chalmers Mitchell in the first Whipsnade guidebook as 'a permanent addition to the beauties of England', it also marked the Society's centenary which had been celebrated the previous year.

Whipsnade was revolutionary: not since the farm at Kingston, or King George IV's animal collection at Windsor a century earlier, had so lavish an attempt been made to allow animals to inhabit open parkland in relative freedom. Much of the excavation for roads, animal housing administrative offices and public facilities was undertaken through a government-sponsored scheme which was aimed at alleviating the chronic unemployment of the early thirties. The first animals were presented by the Duke of Bedford, who lived at nearby Woburn Abbey and was the longest-serving President of the Society (1899–1936). The Duke provided Reeves' muntjac, hog deer, Przewalski's horse (a species which His Grace had helped save from extinction) and Chinese water deer. Sir Anthony Wingfield and Mr Alfred Ezra, both members of the Society's Council, also donated large numbers of animals from their private menageries. The Society later purchased the animals from Bostock and Wombwell's Circus Menagerie, including an elephant called Dixie who played the mouth-organ. On being offered coppers by the amused visitor, she would take them in her trunk and place them in her keeper's pocket. Many of the elephants were used for logging within the Park and proved invaluable in moving the heavy materials required for the construction of yet another Lubetkin-designed building, the Elephant House of 1934. A rather different kind of animal, the Whipsnade Lion – another example of Chalmers Mitchell's eye for pubicity – is an idealistic representation of a male African lion, 600 feet/200 metres long and covering an acre of ground, which adorns the chalk escarpment overlooking the Vale of Aylesbury and is lit from time to time.

Whipsnade opened on 23 May 1931, and the reponse from the public was as unexpected as it was encouraging. Over 1,000 visitors were recorded, and on the following Whit Sunday the country lanes in the neighbourhood were totally choked with cars. Whit Monday proved even more of an embarrassment. A sign had to be erected at St Pancras Station advising prospective visitors via Luton, from where there was a special bus service to the Park, that no more tickets were being issued due to the congestion. In the first eight days some 50,000 people had been to marvel at such innovation.

Whipsnade served the British well abroad, too. During the 1936 Berlin Olympics all competitors were obliged to give the Nazi salute, but the British contingent would have none of it. Whilst giving a fair impression of acknowledging the Führer they chanted, not 'Heil Hitler!', but the immortal phrase: 'Whipsnade, Whipsnade, Zoo, Zoo, Zoo!'

AFFLUENCE BETWEEN THE WARS

The late thirties are generally regarded as the heyday of London Zoo. Annual attendences regularly approached 2 million, with over half a million at Whipsnade. Public transport reigned supreme. Under the auspices of the newly formed London Transport, the greatest city in the world, centre of the British Empire, was served by the most efficient and integrated transport system that the world had ever seen. Trams to Camden Town, Northern

Line to Camden Town, Bakerloo Line to Regent's Park – no wonder that the provision of car parking at London Zoo was not considered for another fifty years. Many of the shopkeepers in Camden's Town Parkway owed their livelihood to Zoo-bound pedestrians calling in for cigarettes, sweets or stale buns with which to feed the elephants.

The Society's Annual Report for 1938 showed an attendance of 1.8 million, a reduction of 6 per cent on the previous year. This was attributed to the 'disturbed international situation'. Whipsnade showed a similar fall, to 523,000. The Report noted that three giant pandas, 'Tang (male), Sung (male thought at first to be female) and Ming (female thought at first to be male)' had been brought from China, a white snub-nosed monkey and a Chinese marmot were also new to the collection. A maned wolf had been purchased from South America and a young orang-utan had been received in exchange for a Mongolian wild horse bred at Whipsnade. Six Galapagos penguins and a king penguin had been presented by Tommy Sopwith of America's Cup fame. Notable births included litters of tigers and leopards. Although two young female cheetahs had been introduced to two males in the hope that they might breed, it would be another 28 years before Whipsnade achieved the distinction of becoming the first British zoo to breed cheetahs. (The Park's record is now second to none: some 120 cubs have been born since the first birth in 1966.)

The Children's Zoo at Regent's Park was opened in 1938 by Robert and Teddy Kennedy, the young sons of US Ambassador Joseph Kennedy. This was the brainchild of Chalmers Mitchell's successor as Secretary of the Society, Sir Julian Huxley. An additional charge of 1s (5p) was made for the Children's Zoo, and some of the earliest visitors were the Princesses Elizabeth and Margaret Rose. The Gardens were floodlit on Wednesday and Thursday evenings during the summer, and did not close until 11pm. The band of the Royal Artillery was engaged to play for the season. Dr David Seth-Smith, the Superintendent, began to make regular appearances on the new medium of television, having established his broadcasting credentials as 'The Zoo Man' in a series of BBC radio programmes. The Zoo magazine, started in 1936, was maintaining a circulation of 100,000.

The Report of 1938 also details the quantities of food consumed by the animals during the year, including 156.5 tons of clover, 21.5 bushels of shrimps, 7,200 lbs of unsweetened condensed milk and 9 tons of monkey nuts; also seven heads of celery and just 14 lbs of prunes, no doubt to relieve constipation. The collection contained 3,624 animals (excluding fishes and invertebrates), of which 233 had been born in the Zoo during the year. At Whipsnade there were 1,725 animals, of which 96 had been bred in the Park. The Society's accounts for the year showed an accumulated surplus of £215,404. No wonder plans were in hand to build a new Elephant House, develop Whipsnade further and consolidate many of the other attractions through the purchase, exchange or even capture of animals. The Society was affluent. It had survived the Depression and there was little competition from other forms of entertainment. It had a settled and dedicated staff, and to be a Fellow of the Zoological Society was an accolade that became *de rigueur* for the man about town. The letters FZS after a name meant something.

THE ZOO AT WAR

On the outbreak of the Second World War on 3 September 1939 the most valuable and rare books from the library, together with the *Daily Occurrences*, a unique record of the Society's activities compiled every day since the founding of the Zoo, were taken to Woburn Abbey. The three giant pandas and Bar-Bar the baby elephant, together with the zebra and elephants, were sent to Whipsnade. All the poisonous snakes and the black widow spiders, which had only recently been the subject of anxious questions in Parliament, were put down. The Children's Zoo was closed. Most of the tanks in the Aquarium were drained and the majority of the fish, other than the rare specimens, were destroyed. George, the centenarian alligator and firm favourite of the staff and public, was retained. Both London Zoo and Whipsnade closed only temporarily, reopening a few days later.

Yet despite these necessary precautions the Society was determined to keep the zoos going even at this difficult time. The 1941 Annual Report stated that 'The policy is to preserve the bulk of the collection. Apart from the national service which it feels it is rendering, in keeping places of healthy recreation available to Fellows, war workers, members of the armed forces and the general public, it considers that it is in the best interests of the Society to prepare for the speediest possible resumption of full activity after the war.' But staffing had to be reduced by 50 per cent, both as an economy measure and due to conscription. Many of the flower beds were used for growing vegetables and pigs were kept in various corners of the Zoo. The carnivores were fed horse meat. By this means, it was hoped to avoid a repeat of the First World War complaint that the animals were receiving better food than that available to the public. Much of the spare land at Whipsnade was ploughed to provide crops of wheat, carrots, potatoes and clover.

Serving members of the armed forces, together with their families, were admitted for half price from 1940, and on Sundays servicemen were admitted free of charge. That year a National Wartime Utility Exhibition was staged in the Zoo with the active encouragement of the Ministry of Agriculture. Daily demonstrations were held on keeping poultry, breeding pigs and goats, beekeeping and the upkeep of allotments. During the Blitz the Zoo suffered its fair share of bomb damage. The Hippo, Monkey and Reptile Houses were all hit, although the major problem was broken glass. Few animals were involved, although at Whipsnade a young giraffe and some antelopes died of shock.

The Society survived the war relatively intact. Returning servicemen were encouraged by the Society to bring back snakes, lizards, birds and small rodents, whose numbers were now depleted due to wartime necessities. Five expeditions were organised to restock the collection; they provided penguins from the Falkland Islands, elephants, giraffes, leopards, cheetahs and tree hyraxes from East Africa, and three young elephants from India. Such expeditions actually continued right through to the 1960s, when the young David Attenborough cut his television teeth with the famous *Zoo Quest* programmes which featured his expeditions to South America and West Africa. In May 1946 a young giant panda called Ma Teh was flown from Szechuan in China in only six days and given quarters in the Lion House, where she soon became a firm favourite with the public. By the end of 1947, the number of animals in the Society's collection was more than double that of 1944.

Shortages of materials and exotic foots were, however, continuing to be a problem since rationing was still in force. Bananas and oranges had to be replaced by carrots and potatoes and many war-damaged buildings could be no more than patched up. The appointment in 1947 of a full-time architect reflected the Society's wish, when finance and materials allowed, to resume building new and ever more imaginative structures. After all, nothing of any significance had been built for over 20 years. Attendances soared. The Zoo was seen as an ideal escape from post-war austerity – what better than to toddle off to see the animals?

STAR ATTRACTIONS

The bumper year of 1950 had the highest ever annual attendance: 3,013,571 people visited London Zoo and a commendable 510,875 at Whipsnade, bearing in mind that petrol was still rationed. The most popular attraction was a young polar bear called Brumas, who had been born at London Zoo the previous year. 'Brumas Fever' spread through the country in much the same way as in 1939 when the arrival of the giant pandas caught the imagination of the press and the public.

Such animal stars have been a feature of the Zoo since its earliest days. Indeed, one of the very first birds in the collection was named Dr Brookes after its donor, the proprietor of a school of anatomy in Blenheim Street. Obaysch was a young hippopotamus presented in 1849 to Queen Victoria by the Viceroy of Egypt – possibly the first hippopotamus seen in Great Britain and the first in Europe since Roman times. He remained an enduring attraction for for 27 years and 'The Hippo Polka' became a popular tune of the day. Obaysch fathered several young, including one named Guy Fawkes, subsequently identified as a female, because he was born in the grounds on 5 November. The first hippopotamus to be reared in captivity by its mother, Guy Fawkes lived in the Zoo until 1908. The first sealion was exhibited in 1866, together with the French sailor named Lecomte who had caught the animal in the Falklands. He was an out-and-out showman, famed for sitting in the middle of the Sealion Pond and feeding the animals in a way that exploited their natural balancing skills.

In 1865 the then Superintendent, A D Bartlett, arranged an exchange of animals with the Jardin des Plantes. The Paris Zoo received a rhinoceros and in exchange sent a young male African elephant. Bartlett named him Jumbo, after a Zulu word meaning 'a large packet'. He would grow into the most famous animal in the world, lending his name to any item synonymous with bulk – aircraft and the ubiquitous burger are just two examples. Jumbo was entrusted to a former keeper of antelopes, Matthew Scott, and the animal soon became tame, allowing up to six children to be carried on his back at a time. But over the years Jumbo's temperament deteriorated and, fearful of an accident, Bartlett decided to sell him. A price of £2,000 was agreed with Phineas T Barnum, the American showman, but the Society's Council had not taken into account the public's reaction to the loss of their favourite animal. Letters were sent to the *Times*, court injunctions sought to prohibit the sale, questions were asked by learned counsel concerning the Council's authority to sell assets, popular songs were published and public petitions raised in an attempt to persuade the Council to change its mind.

But it was all to no avail. Jumbo crossed the Atlantic and began a new life as a star attraction in Barnum's 'Greatest Show on Earth'. In 1885, he was returning to his quarters after a performance in the ring when he was hit by a railway locomotive travelling on an adjacent track to the one housing Jumbo's specially constructed wagon, and died shortly afterwards. The sad news was telegraphed throughout the world.

It is difficult to know exactly why some animals are adopted by the public and yet others, even of the same species, can live all their lives in relative obscurity. Winnie the Pooh was an American black bear presented to the Society in 1914. Immortalised by the author A A Milne, he died of old age in 1934. A plaque behind the Reptile House records Winnie's life. Goldie was a golden eagle who achieved fame by repeatedly escaping in 1969. There have been some eight giant pandas at the Zoo, of whom, unfortunately, none have produced offspring. Perhaps the most famous was Chi Chi, bought by Granada Television and deposited in the Zoo in 1957. His trips to mate with the female giant panda in Moscow Zoo hit the headlines. Guy was a lowland gorilla who arrived from Paris Zoo in 1947. Adult male gorillas were then a rarity in zoos, and he became a firm favourite until his death whilst undergoing surgery in 1978.

NEW RESOURCES, NEW BUILDINGS

Coronation year, 1953, coincided with the 125th anniversary of the opening of the Zoological Gardens in Regent's Park. The Zoo was badly run down. There were still shortages of materials and skilled labour, yet considerable efforts were made to attract visitors to the Zoo during this special year. A coronation collection of animals from the Commonwealth was arranged, and during the summer the Zoo was floodlit in the evenings.

Later, the first comprehensive building plan for the Gardens was produced; the principal contributor was Sir Hugh Casson. The plan envisaged an expansion of the Zoo into Regent's Park in order to soften the boundary, provision for which was eventually obtained in the Crown Estates Act, 1961. The first work to be carried out comprised the refurbishing of Decimus Burton's Giraffe House and the building of a complementary range of ungulate houses, later referred to as the Cotton Terraces in recognition of their principal donor, Sir Jack Cotton. The Terraces were opened by the then President of the Society, Prince Philip, on 16 May 1963. The Northern Aviary was built on the north bank of the Regent's Canal. It was later renamed the Snowdon Aviary in recognition of the Earl of Snowdon, who had been instrumental in drawing together the team of civil engineers, structural specialists and ornithologists responsible for it. The aviary, consisting of a series of tensioned cables anchored to tetrahedral frames covered in mesh, remains one of the largest examples of aluminium construction in the world and is an icon to devotees of the sixties.

The Elephant House of 1965, designed by Sir Hugh Casson, received much praise and many awards from the architectural press, not necessarily endorsed by those who had to tend the animals housed in it. Not to be upstaged by his entrepreneurial rival Jack Cotton, Sir Charles Clore agreed to finance a Small Mammal House; on seeing the plans for the novel incorporation of a nocturnal display, he increased his donation to £200,000. Situated in the Middle Gardens on the site of the old Elephant House, the Small Mammal House featured zoned air conditioning and relied on artificial lighting to enhance the public's appreciation of these creatures and their habitats. It was opened by the Queen in 1967.

The Sobell Pavilions for Apes and Monkeys were financed with a donation of £250,000 from Sir Michael Sobell, the TV manufacturer. The Lion Terraces of 1976, again opened by the Queen, reflected a move to more realistic displays. The impressive use of water, plate glass and ha-has (concealed ditches), enable visitors to enjoy a largely uninterrupted view of the big cats.

INTO THE FUTURE

As long ago as 1870 a statement was made to the House of Commons that 'the Society [was] performing a function that in most civilised countries is undertaken by the state, or materially assisted by grants from the national purse'. However, the Society has always been rather jealous of its independence and was concerned that acceptance of public money would place constraints on its operation. But times change, and over the years the Zoo has needed to accept grants in order to stay afloat.

By 1987, with annual visitor numbers now down to 1.4 million and no new building having been undertaken for 11 years, together with a decaying infrastructure, the future looked bleak. A consultants' report prepared by KPMG Peat Marwick recommended that the Zoo should no longer be operated by the mainly research-oriented Council. It also highlighted the fact that the increase in overseas travel, the growth of theme parks in the UK and higher expectations on the part of visitors could only be met by a radical overhaul. A separate company was established to run both London and Whipsnade, and a business plan was produced in the hope of attracting funding from the private sector. The government provided a grant of £10 million.

The managing director of the new company was Andy Grant, an American who had achieved considerable success with San Diego Zoo in California and Leeds Castle in Kent. He proposed to utilise the Society's assets by a series of innovative schemes including a *son et lumière* presentation centred on the Regent's Canal and telling the story of Noah and the Flood. He also thought that the time was right to activate the proposal to expand the Zoo into Regent's Park, despite local fears of a Disney-style theme park. But corporate money was not forthcoming in the face of this hostility.

Matters grew worse. Old, internal conflicts between the scientific aims of the Society and its running of the country's premier wildlife attraction began to surface. A deepening depression nationally, coupled with decreasing gate receipts, meant that deficits increased. In 1990 London Zoo lost £1.8 million and Whipsnade £970,000. The next year was little better. Despite sustained pressure on the Government, no further cash was offered. In order to protect other aspects of the Society, particularly Whipsnade, its major asset, drastic action needed to be taken to stem the losses at London Zoo – which was, after all, only leased from the Crown. The *Sunday Times* ran a leaked story that the Zoo was going to close.

'Save our Zoo' caught on, and the public rallied round: some £350,000 was donated in two months. A cost-cutting exercise was undertaken, and the new, slim-line set-up indicated that London Zoo was just about viable. But revenue and visitor numbers obstinately refused to increase at anything like the speed needed for recovery.

Meeting at Whipsnade in June 1992, in the light of a disastrous Easter and poor spring attendances, Council resolved to close London Zoo at the end of the summer season. Only one member opposed the motion. Staff were put on notice, and arrangements made to rehouse most of the important animals. Despite the growth in recent years of factions opposed to zoos, there was overwhelming public sympathy for the Society's predicament. A leader in *The Times* was followed by a four-hour documentary on BBC TV, and a host of celebrities joined the fight to keep the Zoo. A report from the House of Commons Select Committee for the Environment came out in support of the Society, and admonished the government for its long-term failure to help the Society keep up its listed buildings. Overseas zoo directors responded, bombarding the government with pleas for compassion, and comparing Britain's situation with their own generous public funding. In July 1992 the Emir of Kuwait gave London Zoo £1 million 'as a gift from the children of Kuwait to the children of London' in recognition of the part played by UK forces in the Gulf War. This gift, more than any other, made the Council reconsider its earlier decision to close. It gave the Zoo hope.

It was the architectural writer Ian Nairn who referred to London Zoo as Noah's Ark and the Tower of Babel combined. There are ten listed buildings in the Zoo grounds, and it lies within the Regent's Park conservation area. Statutory and ethical requirements place ever-increasing demands on it, yet in spite of all this London Zoo remains to this day one of the world's truly great zoos, fulfilling an even more important role in education and conservation than could have been envisaged by its founding fathers nearly two centuries ago. Long may it continue to do so.

Zoo
S T C Weeks
1913
40 × 25in/101.6 × 63.5cm

This strong image is the Underground's first pictorial poster to advertise the Zoo.
The first station name to appear on a Zoo poster was Camden Town. Two years later the second poster suggested that visitors should travel to the Zoo via Regent's Park or Camden Town.

Off to the Zoo
Reginald Rigby
1915
40 × 25in/101.6 × 63.5cm

Although the First World War had already started, the Underground continued to promote leisure travel, often with a strong sense of humour.

For the Zoo
Senota
1915
40 × 25in/101.6 × 63.5cm

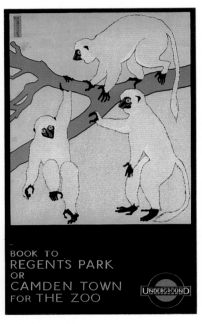

Book to Regent's Park
Dorothy Burroughes
1920
40 × 25in/101.6 × 63.5cm

For the Zoo
Anonymous
1920
40 × 25in/101.6 × 63.5 cm

The decorative animals and ark forming the border of this simple but effective poster are based on a child's toy ark. Seventy-three years later, in Rachel Widdows' poster (page 90), the ark was seen no longer as a toy but as a symbol of refuge for, and a way of saving from extinction, the world's many threatened species.

Happy Days at the Zoo
M Jackson
1922
Issued by
London County Council Tramways
28.5 × 14.25in/72.4 × 36.8cm

A female Asiatic elephant in the 19th century was probably the first to give rides, always a very popular attraction at the Zoo, until they ceased in the early 1960s.

London Characters – The Zoo Keeper
E A Cox
1920
30 × 20in/76.2 × 50.8 cm

This poster of a zoo keeper with his parrot was one of a series of 12 by Cox showing 'typical' Londoners at work. Others in the series included a Covent Garden Porter, a Bus Conductor and a Flower Seller. Although these posters were popular in their time, Cox's style appears old-fashioned today. This is the only poster which gives prominence to a member of the Zoo's staff.

E·A·COX·

LONDON CHARACTERS

THE ZOO KEEPER
- BOOK TO -
REGENTS PARK
or CAMDEN TOWN
- FOR THE ZOO -

FOR THE ZOO, BOOK TO REGENT'S PARK OR CAMDEN TOWN

Sanders Phillips & Co., Ltd., The Baynard Press, London, S.W.9

For the Zoo
Book to Regent's Park
Charles Paine
1921
40 × 25in/101.6 × 63.5cm

This bold graphic design, typical of Paine's style, has been a perennial favourite and reproductions of it continue to sell well.

For the Zoo
Dorothy Burroughes
1922
40 × 25in/101.6 × 63.5cm

For the Zoo
John Platt
1922
40 × 25in/101.6 × 63.5cm

Today London Transport's roundel is well known and respected but over the years different logos have appeared. The example on this poster was only used for a short period in the 1920s. The coat of arms on the left represents the crest of the City of London, while that on the right represents Westminster.

FOR THE ZOO

TRAVEL BY

LONDON'S UNDERGROUND

ALIGHT AT CAMDEN TOWN OR
REGENTS PARK STATIONS

I Am at the Zoo
Bring Me a Fly
Martin Pollock
1923
40 × 25in/101.6 × 63.5cm

Regent's Park for the Zoo
Barraclough
1923
40 × 25in/101.6 × 63.5cm

This is the only poster which advertises the Botanic Gardens in Regent's Park as well as the Zoo.

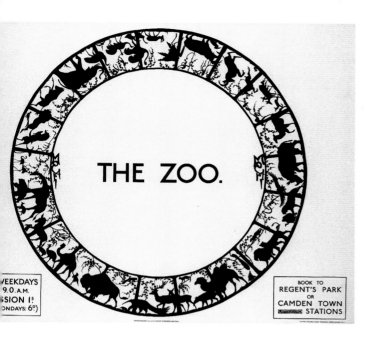

The Zoo
Ugo Mochi
1923
40 × 50in/101.6 × 127cm

This unusual but striking treatment,
although typical of Mochi's work,
is not as successful as some of his
other posters.

Camden Town for the Zoo
Mary I Wright
1924
Issued by
London County Council Tramways
28.5 × 14.25in/72.4 × 36.8cm

This was one of a set of 12 posters
designed by students at London
County Council's Central School of
Arts and Crafts for the LCC's
tramways. It was also issued as a four
sheet poster (40 × 60in/101.6 ×
152.4cm).

The Zoo
F Gregory Brown
1924
40 × 25in/101.6 × 63.5cm

F Gregory Brown was among the
most prolific artists working for the
Underground: he designed 61
posters, three of which advertised
the Zoo.

Camden Town for the Zoo
F W C Farleigh
1924
Issued by
London County Council Tramways
28.5 × 14.25in/72.4 × 36.8cm

This rather confusing picture of
fishes was also issued as a poster in
the much larger 60 × 40in/152.4 ×
101.6cm format. F W Farleigh, later
to sign himself as John Farleigh,
achieved fame for his illustration of
Shaw's *The Black Girl in Search of
God*, and was to design posters for
London Transport right up until his
death in 1965.

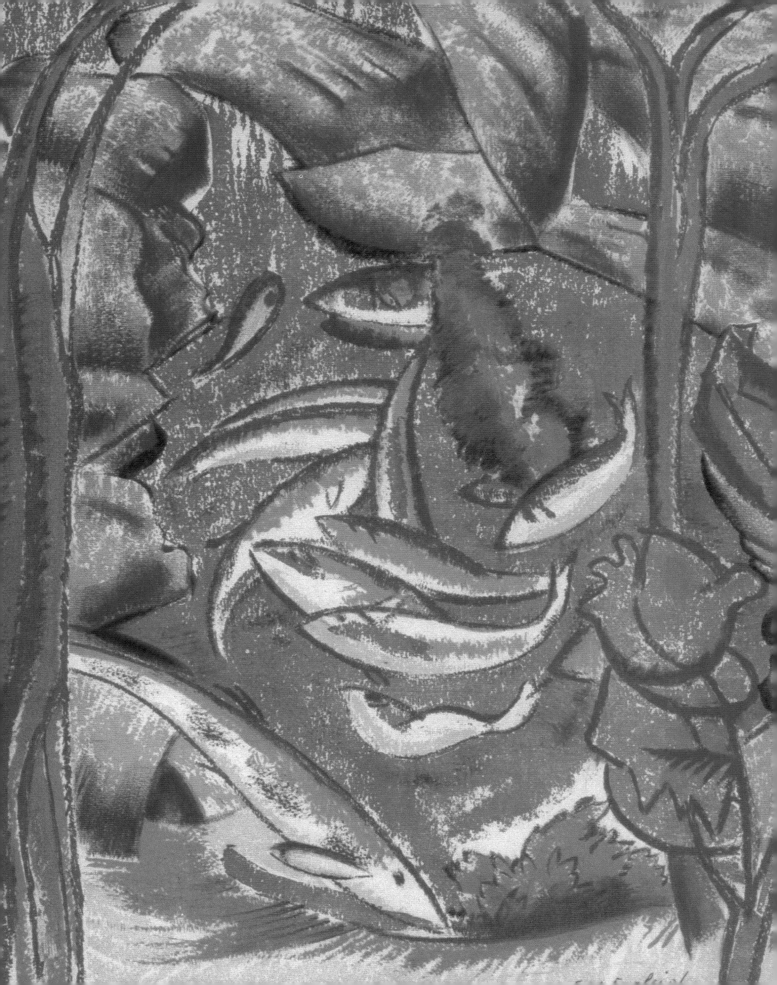

The New Aquarium Now Open
George Sheringham
1924
40 × 25in/101.6 × 63.5cm

The opening in 1924 of the new aquarium, designed by Joass, was a major event. Over the years it featured on at least nine posters, a surprisingly high number considering the wealth of other interesting subjects available at the Zoo.

Take Them to the Zoo
James H Dowd
1924
40 × 25in/101.6 × 63.5cm

J.H. DOWD

TAKE THEM TO
THE ZOO

BOOK TO REGENT'S PARK OR CAMDEN TOWN

Nº 1377 - 2,000 - 4/10/24   THE DANGERFIELD PRINTING Cº LᵀᴰLONDON

For the Zoo – Sealion
Ruth Sandys
1925
40 × 25in/101.6 × 63.5cm

At the Zoo – Leopard
Artist unknown
1925
40 × 25in/101.6 × 63.5cm

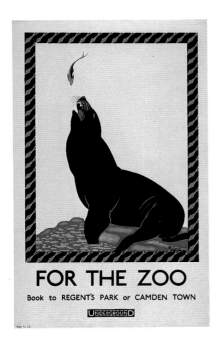

The Zoo – Fish
Gwynedd M Hudson
1926
40 × 25in/101.6 × 63.5cm

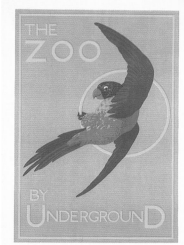

The Zoo – Parrot
D Barry
1926
40 × 25in/101.6 × 63.5cm

The Zoo – Parrots
Van Jones
1927
Issued by
London County Council Tramways
28.5 × 14.25in/72.4 × 36.8cm

The Chimpanzees Request the Pleasure
of Your Company
Photographer unknown
1927
11.5 × 18.25in/29.2 × 46.4cm

Chimpanzees' tea parties were first
held in 1927 and ran for 45 years,
when they were stopped because it
was believed that it was demeaning
for them.

The Zoo – Monkeys
Edmunds
1928
Issued by
London County Council Tramways
30 × 20in/76.2 × 50.8cm

It is hoped that the spelling of
Camden Town was corrected before
publication! This artwork was
designed to be enlarged to make a
four sheet poster
(40 × 60in/101.6 × 152.4cm).

Zoo - Kangaroos
F Gregory Brown
1927
40 × 25in/101.6 × 63.5cm

A New Chart of the Zoo
Herry Perry
1927
40 × 25in/101.6 × 63.5cm

This map may have been an accurate representation of the Zoo, but its purpose could only have been as a decorative advertisement since it would have been on display inside Underground stations. Herry Perry usually recorded her work as being finished on the eve of a saint's day. This is no exception.

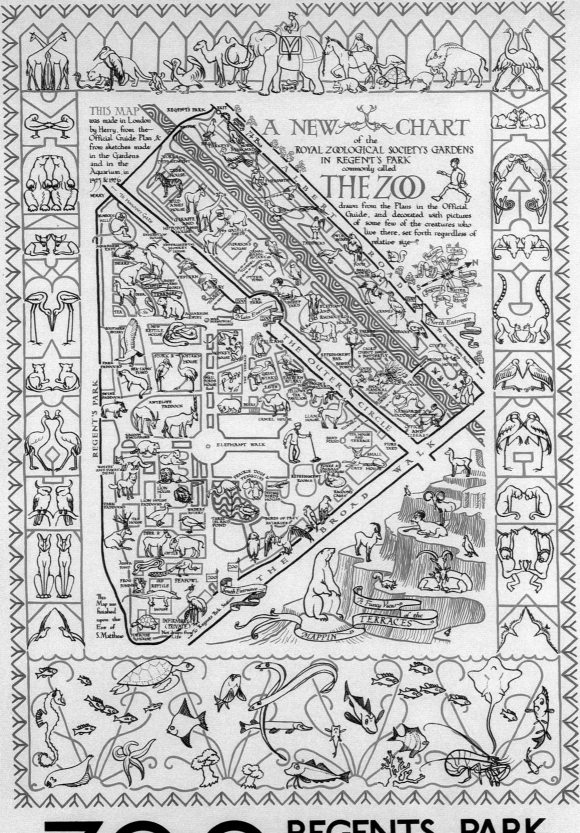

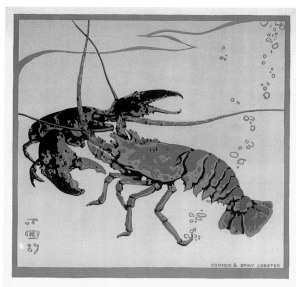

Zoo – Common and Spiny Lobster
R B Talbot Kelly
1927
40 × 25in/101.6 × 63.5cm

The Zoo – Goats
Clive Gardiner
1927
40 × 25in/101.6 × 63.5cm

The design of this poster was influenced by the Cubist movement. Unfortunately the mountain terraces, which form the subject of this poster, are now closed. It is hoped that they will reopen when funds permit.

ive Gardiner

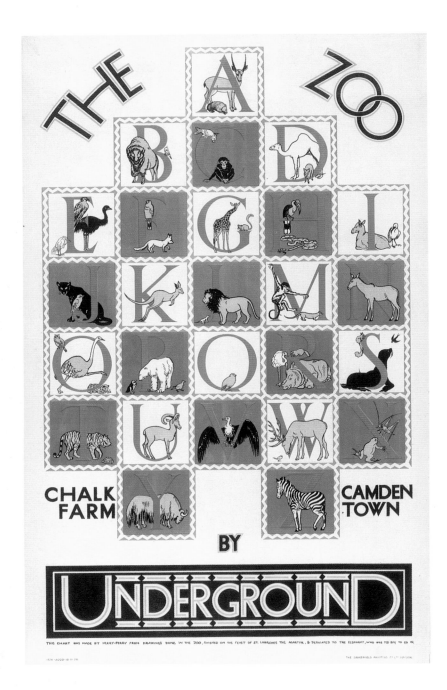

Living Pictures at the Zoo
Small
1928
40 × 25in/101.6 × 63.5cm

The title of this poster had appeared the previous year in the wording of Gardiner's poster 'The Zoo – Goats' (page 46 (right)).

The Zoo Alphabet
Herry Perry
1928
40 × 25in/101.6 × 63.5cm

The first Underground poster to use the alphabet as a basis for its design and subject was issued in 1915. This was the fourth and last attempt at using the idea.

At the Zoo
– The Man-Eater Just Arrived
Photographer Topical Press Agency
1929
12.75 × 9.75in/32.4 × 24.3cm

See the Zoo
Harold Stabler
1930
40 × 50in/101.6 × 127cm

The way the individual animals have been compartmentalised in this poster forces one to concentrate on the detail of the drawing rather than the overall picture, perhaps reflecting Stabler's work as a ceramicist and sculptor. He designed many of the decorative tiles that appear on the Underground.

Zoo – Toucans
Tony Castle
1929
Issued by
London County Council Tramways
28.5 × 14.25in/72.4 × 36.8cm

Zoo – Leopard
P Irwin Brown
1930
Issued by
London County Council Tramways
30 × 20in/76.2 × 50.8cm

The pencil notes on the artwork
confirm that this was to be used for
a four sheet poster.

Zoo – Lion Cub
M K Mountain
1930
Issued by
London County Council Tramways
28.5 × 14.25in/72.4 × 36.8cm

These photographic panel posters
show three of the latest arrivals at
the Zoo. Elizabeth and Gus were
sold in 1930 and 1931 respectively,
with only Lerline remaining.
African lions are no longer kept at
the Zoo, but have been replaced by
the much rarer Asiatic lion.

I Am Lerline
– Waiting for You at the Zoo
Photographer Kingston
1930
12.75 × 9.75in/32.4 × 24.3cm

I Am Elizabeth
– Waiting for You at the Zoo
Photographer Kingston
1930
12.75 × 9.75in/32.4 × 24.3cm

I Am Gus
– Waiting for You at the Zoo
Photographer Kingston
1930
12.75 × 9.75in/32.4 × 24.3cm

From the Ark to Regent's Park
Arnrid Johnston
1931
40 × 60in/101.6 × 127cm

This 'political' poster refers to the
Development (Loan Guarantees and
Grants) Act which was passed in
1929, allowing the Treasury to
guarantee approved public utility
works. These included several
Underground projects.

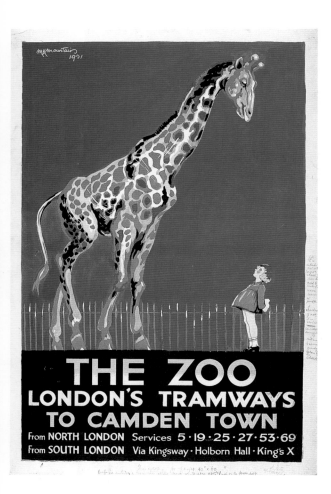

The Zoo – Giraffe
M K Mountain
1931
Issued by
London County Council Tramways
30 × 20in/76.2 × 50.8cm

Detailed pencil notes in the margins
of the original design recommend
necessary changes in colour to the
giraffe and the girl's cheeks.

The Zoo – Aquarium
F Gregory Brown
1931
40 × 25in/101.6 × 63.5cm

The Zoo – Flamingos
Frank Marsden Lea
1932
Issued by
London County Council Tramways
28.5 × 14.25in/72.4 × 36.8cm

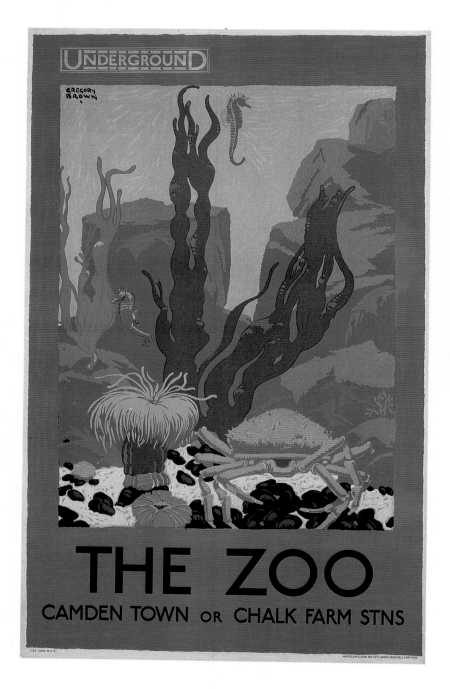

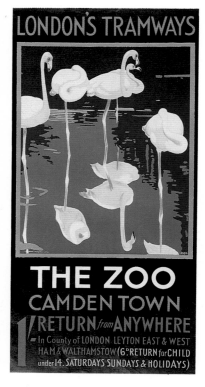

ANK=MARSDEN=LEA

1932

The Zoo – Parrots
Lawson Wood
1932
Issued by
London County Council Tramways
28.5 × 14.25in/72.4 × 36.8cm

Whipsnade
Arnrid Johnston
1932
40 × 25in/101.6 × 63.5cm

This was the first Underground
poster to promote Whipsnade Zoo,
which had opened the previous
year. It attempts to illustrate the
relative freedom of the animals in
Whipsnade's 600 acres, compared to
the confined spaces at London Zoo.

Orpheus at Whipsnade
Herry Perry
1933
40 × 25in/101.6 × 63.5cm

Another poster by this prolific artist,
this time loosely based on the
ancient Greek myth of Orpheus,
whose music was said to be
irresistible not just to people but also
to animals and even to stones.

Zoo – Bath Time
Lawson Wood
1933
Issued by
London County Council Tramways
28.5 × 14.25in/72.4 × 36.8cm

This comic poster, along with that on page 60 (left), appears to belittle the animals shown, in stark contrast to the more dignified treatment found in even London Transport's humorous posters such as the ones on pages 21 and 81.

The Zoo – Lemur
Oleg Zinger
1933
40 × 25in/101.6 × 63.5cm

There's a Transport of Joy at the Zoo
Jean Dupas
1933
40 × 25in/101.6 × 63.5cm

1933 saw the formation of the London Passenger Transport Board, whose short-lived symbol appears in this poster.

"There's a
Transport of Joy at the Zoo."

Camden Town, Chalk Farm or Regents Park "Underground" Stn.

Visit the Zoo
– By Tram to Camden Town
Artist unknown
1934
20.3 × 8.3in/51.4 × 21cm

This comes from a much larger series of letterpress posters in the same style, all with decorative margins. Another poster suggested travel to Edgware Road for the Zoo, while sporting events were also heavily promoted.

For the Zoo
Maurice A Miles
1934
40 × 25in/101.6 × 63.5cm

Little is known about this artist's work. He designed two posters for the Underground – one for the Zoo, the other for Kew Gardens.

The Komodo Dragon
Photographer Howard Coster
1934
10 × 12in/25.4 × 30.5cm

Small panel posters such as this were popular in the 1930s. This size appeared on the glass screens immediately inside the doors on the tube trains. The Zoo's two Komodo Dragons became so tame that children could be left safely with them.

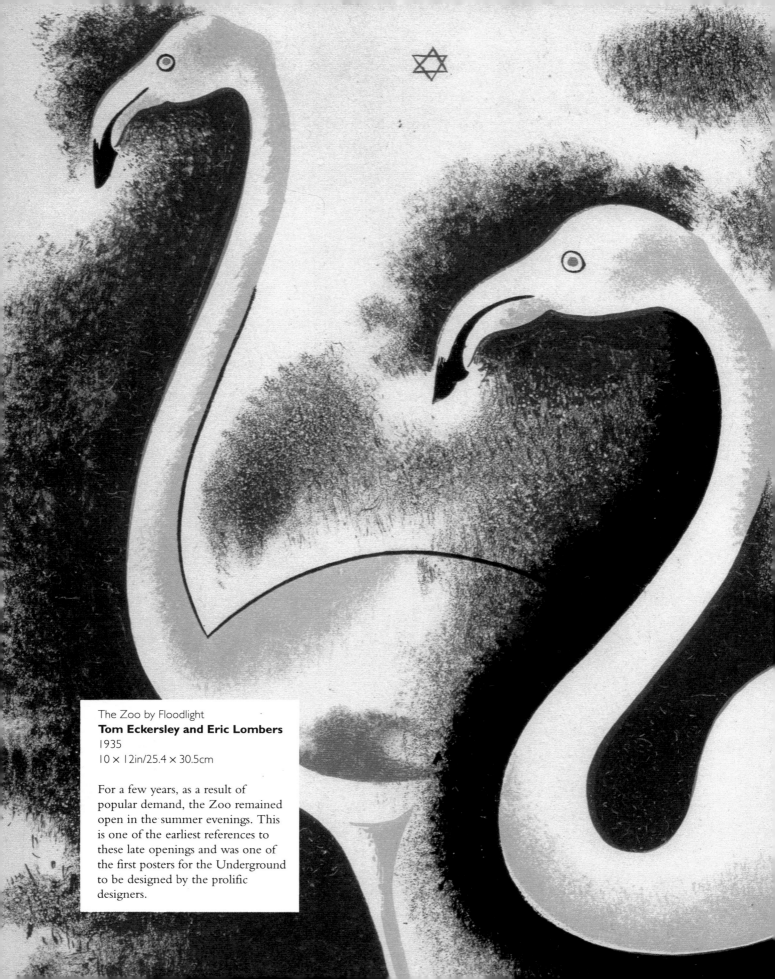

The Zoo by Floodlight
Tom Eckersley and Eric Lombers
1935
10 × 12in/25.4 × 30.5cm

For a few years, as a result of
popular demand, the Zoo remained
open in the summer evenings. This
is one of the earliest references to
these late openings and was one of
the first posters for the Underground
to be designed by the prolific
designers.

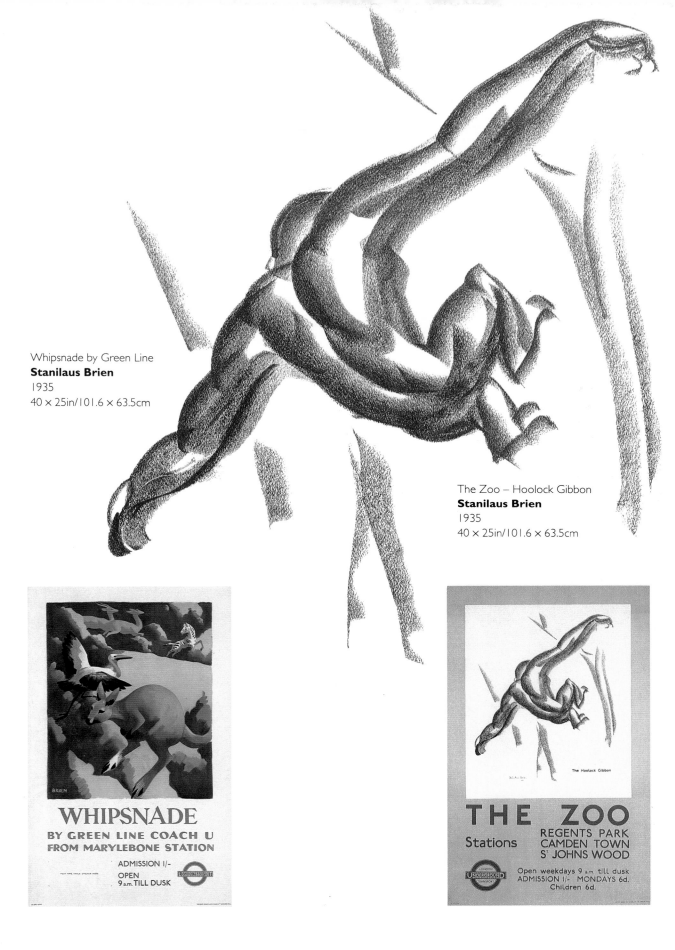

Whipsnade by Green Line
Stanilaus Brien
1935
40 × 25in/101.6 × 63.5cm

The Zoo – Hoolock Gibbon
Stanilaus Brien
1935
40 × 25in/101.6 × 63.5cm

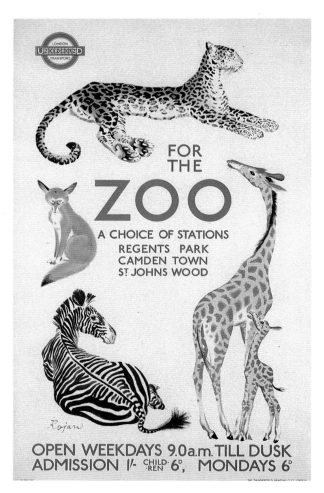

For the Zoo
Rojan
1935
40 × 25in/101.6 × 63.5cm

This poster advertised London Transport's Underground services, while another version advertised the company's tramway services to the Zoo. For the latter, the small roundel in the top left-hand corner was replaced with one saying 'Tramways'.

Zoo – Chameleon
Oleg Zinger
1935
40 × 25in/101.6 × 63.5cm

Zoo Nights
Clifford Ellis and Rosemary Ellis
1936
10 × 12in/25.4 × 30.5cm

ZOO

STATIONS

REGENTS PARK
CAMDEN TOWN
ST JOHNS WOOD

BUS ROUTE No 74

WHIPSNADE

Cheap day return THROUGH tickets
are now issued daily to Whipsnade
from St. Pancras and other LMS stations
via St. Albans City station
and thence by 368 (Green) Bus

Ask for handbill at Ticket Office

Whipsnade
Michael Ross
1936
40 × 25in/101.6 × 63.5cm

This view of the wolves, today the
largest pack in England, is similar
today to the way it was in the 1930s
although the wolves have actually
been relocated to another paddock.

WHIPSNADE ZOO BY THIS BUS

Whipsnade Zoo by this Bus
Zero (Hans Schleger)
1937
10 × 28.5in/25.4 × 72.4cm

This must be the only pictorial
poster of either zoo which does not
show a single animal. In fact this
image, which would have appeared
inside the saloon of a bus, was used
to advertise a multitude of
destinations around London.

Indoor Zoo
Richard Beck
1937
40 × 25in/101.6 × 63.5cm

Now He's at the Zoo
John Barker (Kraber)
1938
40 × 25in/101.6 × 63.5cm

3 Ways to Whipsnade
R Knight
1937
40 × 25in/101.6 × 63.5cm

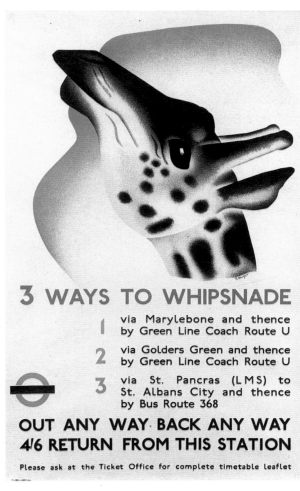

Zoo Nights
H Blacker
1939
10 × 12in/25.4 × 30.5cm

Giant Panda
Clifford Ellis and Rosemary Ellis
1939
10 × 12in/25.4 × 30.5cm

In late 1938 the Zoo bought three pandas, originally named Grumpy, Dopey and Baby after the dwarfs in Walt Disney's *Snow White and the Seven Dwarfs*. They were later renamed Sung, Tang and Ming. In the spring and summer of 1939 the pandas became a great attraction. Ming Ming, the last Giant Panda, left the Zoo in October 1994 as a result of unsuccessful attempts to breed.

The Zoo – Camel
Bip Pares
1939
40 × 25in/101.6 × 63.5cm

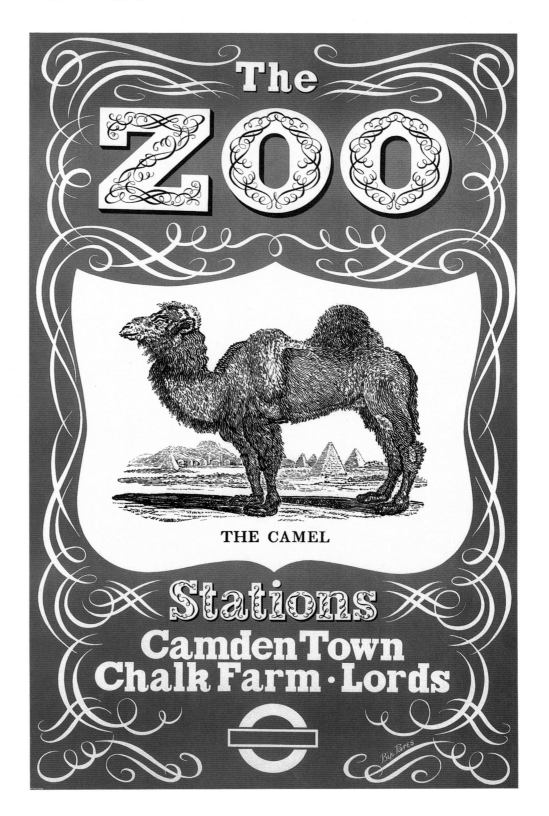

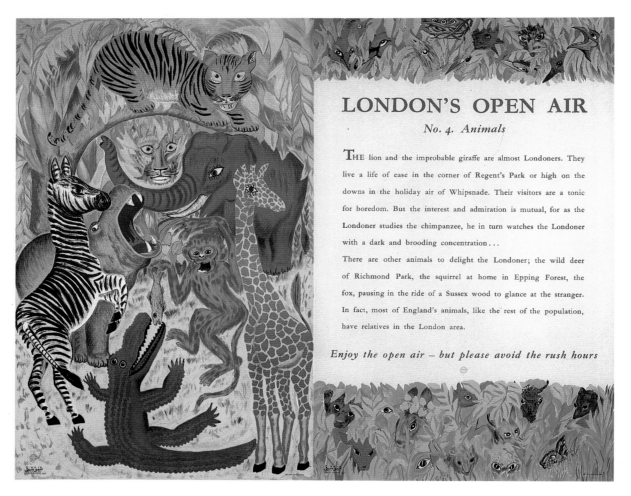

LONDON'S OPEN AIR

No. 4. Animals

THE lion and the improbable giraffe are almost Londoners. They live a life of ease in the corner of Regent's Park or high on the downs in the holiday air of Whipsnade. Their visitors are a tonic for boredom. But the interest and admiration is mutual, for as the Londoner studies the chimpanzee, he in turn watches the Londoner with a dark and brooding concentration...

There are other animals to delight the Londoner; the wild deer of Richmond Park, the squirrel at home in Epping Forest, the fox, pausing in the ride of a Sussex wood to glance at the stranger. In fact, most of England's animals, like the rest of the population, have relatives in the London area.

Enjoy the open air – but please avoid the rush hours

London's Open Air No. 4 Animals
Shafig Shawki
1948
40 × 25in/101.6 × 63.5cm each poster

This is a fine example of the pair poster, in which one half of the poster was given over to the pictorial image while the other half was devoted to text, often very lengthy. This poster was the fourth in a set of six pair posters issued in 1948, each by a different artist. All had the theme of London's Open Air.

Brush Up Your Jungle
William Roberts
1953
35 × 8.5in/89 × 21.6cm

The commissioning of small pictorial posters to fit bus stop panels was common in the 1950s. The title of this poster was inspired by the song 'Brush Up Your Shakespeare' from Cole Porter's musical *Kiss Me Kate*, the MGM film of which was released in the same year as the poster. Other versions of this poster appear with different wording and in different sizes. This is one of the few posters which also advertises Chessington Zoo, now Chessington World of Adventures.

Wild or Savage
Betty Swanwick
1954
40 × 25in/101.6 × 63.5cm each poster

Whipsnade
Hans Unger
1956
25 × 40in/63.5 × 101.6cm

A witty and light-hearted interpretation by this versatile artist. Although suggestive of an urban environment, it is actually advertising Whipsnade. The use of limericks on posters became very popular during the 1950s and 1960s.

A picnic of children from Bow
Was chased by some wolves through the snow
Their mistress and feeder
Machine-gunned the leader

And would have shot a wolf too if she
had taken a Green Line Coach to Whipsnade
which costs 4/3 on route 726 from Baker Street
and studied the vulnerable points of wolves.

The Zoo – Aquarium
Enid Marx
1957
40 × 25in/101.6 × 63.5cm

These two posters are not strictly pair posters, as text and images are mixed. Enid Marx also designed moquette for seating in Underground trains in the 1930s.

OLD NOAH'S love of beasts we know
Was not confined to fur-face.
His plans included tanks to show
The life below the surface.

So, Japheth left to steer the Ark,
And aqualung collected,
Our hero braved the salty dark
And fishy pairs selected.

This ancient submarine delight
Is now a public pleasure,
The Zoo Aquarium is quite
Ideal for winter leisure.

 The best way to the Zoo and its Aquarium at Regent's Park is to go by Underground to Camden Town or Baker Street and then take a 74 bus

Details of times of opening and admission fees are given in a London Transport booklet 'How to Get There' which also gives similar information for some 400 of London's places of interest. It is included free with the guide-book 'Visitor's London' which costs 4/6, or it can be bought separately for 6d. All London Transport publications, including free maps and leaflets, can be obtained from the Travel Enquiry Offices at Piccadilly Circus and St. James's Park Underground stations, or from the Publicity Officer, 55 Broadway, S.W.I.

The Zoo – Noah's Ark
Enid Marx
1957
40 × 25in/101.6 × 63.5cm

Old Noah stocked his sturdy Ark
With animals both old and gnu
And sailed away to Regent's Park
To found a comprehensive Zoo.

To Whipsnade, then, the course was clear
For Shem the navigator,
To start one in the open air
Ideal for the spectator.

The booklet 'How to Get There' cites
Admission fees and when to go
To Zoos and all the other sights
The London visitor should know.

 The best way to the Zoo at Regent's Park is to go by Underground to Camden Town or Baker Street and take a 74 bus to the gate. The best way to Whipsnade is to take a 726 Green Line coach from Baker Street (Allsop Place, just behind the station) direct to the gate. The single fare to Whipsnade is 4/3.

'How to Get There' is a London Transport booklet which lists some 400 of London's places of interest, both famous and less well-known, together with times of opening, prices of admission and how to get there by London Transport. 'How to Get There' is included free with the guide-book 'Visitor's London' which costs 4/6. It can also be bought separately, price 6d. All London Transport publications, including free maps and leaflets, can be obtained from the Publicity Officer, London Transport, 55 Broadway, Westminster, S.W.I.

Zoo Ahoy
John Burningham
1961
40 × 25in/101.6 × 63.5cm

The Zoo Aquarium
Hans Unger and Eberhard Schulze
1963
40 × 25in/101.6 × 63.5cm

Hans Unger collaborated with
the mosaicist Eberhard Schulze
on a number of posters for
London Transport.

WE ANIMALS really are well-off in London. Take the London Zoo – smart new Elephant House, brilliant and unconventional new Aviary (not quite finished), classic-of-modern-architecture Penguin Pool, all in the setting of Nash's Regent's Park. Whipsnade's wide open spaces are high on Dunstable Downs – just like home but safer and very much more comfortable. Chessington is more intimate, and caters specially for children. At all three zoos we welcome visitors. They enjoy themselves. And, of course, they interest and amuse us too . . .

Ask for a free 'Know Your Animals' leaflet at any London Transport Enquiry Office

86

We Animals
Bill Leeson
1965
40 × 25in/101.6 × 63.5cm

This is one of the few posters which also mention London's third zoo at Chessington in Surrey, now Chessington World of Adventures.

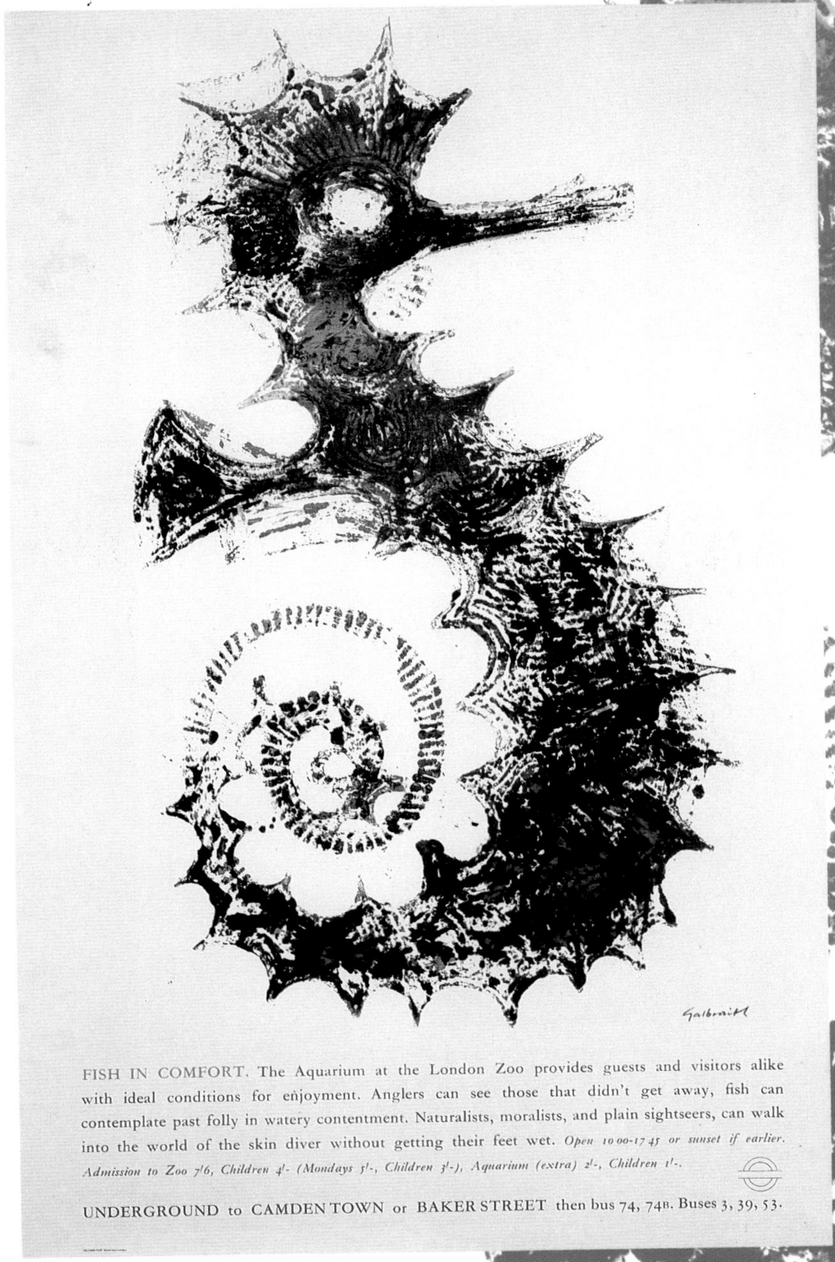

Fish in Comfort
Victor Galbraith
1966
40 × 25in/101.6 × 63.5cm

FISH IN COMFORT. The Aquarium at the London Zoo provides guests and visitors alike with ideal conditions for enjoyment. Anglers can see those that didn't get away, fish can contemplate past folly in watery contentment. Naturalists, moralists, and plain sightseers, can walk into the world of the skin diver without getting their feet wet. *Open 10 00-17 45 or sunset if earlier.*

Admission to Zoo 7/6, Children 4/- (Mondays 5/-, Children 3/-), Aquarium (extra) 2/-, Children 1/-.

UNDERGROUND to CAMDEN TOWN or BAKER STREET then bus 74, 74B. Buses 3, 39, 53.

Zoo Choice – Flamingo
Michael Reid
1970
40 × 25in/101.6 × 63.5cm

This photographic montage shows the award-winning Snowdon aviary.

London Zoo
Abram Games
1976
40 × 25in/101.6 × 63.5cm

This extremely clever and successful interpretation of the subject was the last poster designed by Games for London Transport. Among all the posters promoting the Zoo, this famous designer's work is perhaps the only truly example of pure graphic non-representational art. Cleverly hidden within the figure of the tiger is at least one of London Transport's roundels.

ZOO CHOICE There are several zoos at Regent's Park. There's the one which almost everyone knows (and loves) providing comic monkeys, mendicant strictly not-to-be-fed bears, and camel rides. But there are other, subtler, delights for both sightseer and student — the luminous enamelled treasures of the aquarium, the ungainly flamboyant flamingo, the rainbow host of exquisites who flash, chattering, way above your head within the lacy confines of the Snowdon Aviary. It's your choice; there's something for all tastes and all ages at London Zoo.

Underground to Baker Street or Camden Town, then bus 74.

Do the Zoo
Rachel Widdows
Art on the Underground series
1993
60 × 40in/152.4 × 101.6cm

While a student at the Royal
Academy, Rachel Widdows found
the Zoo provided a wonderful
opportunity to study and draw
animals at close quarters. For the
commission she did for London
Underground she chose to paint a
large, ambitious oil painting
representing the crisis of endangered
species. The artist described her
painting as representing 'the last
stragglers making their way to the
Ark. They move slowly across the
desert in the evening light. Time is
running out but they do not rush,
and unknowingly face the possibility
of extinction. Only we are aware of
their desperate plight.'

NOTES ON ARTISTS

Few commercial artists are well known, and most have had little written about them. Although the London Transport Museum has an almost complete collection of posters produced by London Transport, very few records survive relating to the actual commissioning. The authors would be interested in hearing from anyone with further information about the artists and their work.

Dates at the ends of entries are for the period the artist worked for the London County Council and London Transport.

JOHN ROLAND BARKER 1911–59
Born in Leicestershire, he studied part-time from 1927 to 1932 at Leicester School of Art. In 1932, on a travelling scholarship from the International Guild of Decorators, he visited Italy and Paris. He became a graphic designer in 1934 and was an assistant of Austin Cooper while teaching part-time at Eastbourne School of Art. In 1938 he designed murals for several exhibitions. During the Second World War he served in the navy. In 1950 he won the Poster Competition for the United Kingdom Recovery Programme. During the fifties he held several exhibitions and designed posters, textiles and magazines for Shell, Fisons and ICI among others. Some work from the late 1930s is signed Kraber.
4 posters, 1935–8. Page 75 (left).

BARRACLOUGH
This is possibly James Barraclough (d. 1942), a London-based portrait painter in oils who exhibited at the Royal Academy and Royal Institute of Oil-Painters.
3 posters, 1922–3. Page 30 (right).

D BARRY
1 panel poster, 1926. Page 41 (left).

RICHARD BECK 1912–85
Born in Hampshire, he studied art at the Slade and also in Munich. Before the Second World War Beck had his own design consultancy in London where he designed poster and press advertisements for London Transport, Shell Mex and the Orient Line. During the war he served with the Australian Imperial Force. In the late 1940s he established his own design agency, Richard Beck Associates. During the 1950s he won many awards in Australia for his design work. He was Head of Graphic Design at Prahran Technical College, 1969–72.
6 posters, 1935–8. Page 74 (below).

H BLACKER
2 panel posters, 1938–9. Page 76 (above).

G STANILAUS BRIEN
A lino-cut artist, he also designed two posters for the London and North Eastern Railway.
2 posters, 1935. Pages 68, 69 (below left) and 69 (below right).

F GREGORY BROWN 1887–1948
In 1903 he began his career as an art metalworker, but soon turned to magazine illustration. Brown was a founder member of the Design and Industries Association in 1915, and designed posters for the Empire Marketing Board, ICI, MacFisheries and the four main railway companies. In 1925 he won a gold medal for textile design at the 1925 Paris Exhibition of Decorative Arts.
48 posters, 1916–40; 13 panel posters, 1926–32. Pages 32–33, 34 (left), 44, 55 and 58 (left).

P IRWIN BROWN
He designed posters for the London Midland and Scottish and Great Western Railways, as well as London County Council Tramways.
4 posters for London County Council Tramways, 1928–30. Page 52.

JOHN MACINTOSH BURNINGHAM b. 1936
Born in Farnham, Surrey, he studied at the Central School of Art and Crafts, 1956–9. He won the Kate Greenaway Medal for his first picture book in 1963, since when he has written and illustrated many other books.
7 posters and 2 panel posters, 1961–6. Page 84 (left).

DOROTHY MARY L BURROUGHES d. 1963
She studied at the Slade School and later at Heatherley's School of Fine Art and in Germany before becoming a poster designer and writer and illustrator of books and magazines, specialising in animal and figure subjects. Her books include *Queer Beasts at the Zoo* (1927) and *Queer Birds at the Zoo* (1927).
2 posters, 1920–2. Pages 22 (right) and 28.

TONY CASTLE 1891–1971
He designed a poster for the London and North Eastern Railway, and a number of book jackets.
7 posters for London County Council Tramways, 1927–9. Page 51.

TERRY CHRISTIEN b. 1943
At the age of 15 he started working for Pearl and Dean's cartoon animation studio, which produced work for television and cinema advertising. Whilst there he studied life drawing and calligraphy. He now works in graphic design,

specialising in the use of cartoons for advertising, publishing, audiovisual, TV and film. He is a member of the Cartoonists' Club of Great Britain and the Cartoonists' Guild. 1 leaflet, 1993. Page 96.

ELIJAH ALBERT COX 1876–1955
Born in Islington, North London, he studied at Whitechapel People's Palace and Bolt Court before becoming a mural painter and poster artist. Cox painted in oil, watercolour and pastel, and his posters included work for railway and shipping companies.
He worked as a designer for a manufacturing chemist and later assisted the painter Frank Brangwyn, squaring-up studies for transfer from paper to canvas. He also illustrated a number of books. He exhibited widely at various venues including the Royal Academy and the Society of Graphic Artists, and was elected to the Royal Society of British Artists in 1915 and the Royal Institute of Painters in Watercolours in 1921. He lived in London and Canterbury.
25 posters, 1915–24. Page 25.

CREATIVE DESIGN
Founded by John Walker in the early 1980s, the company has mainly produced design and packaging for the fast-moving consumer goods market. It has built up a reputation as a top-quality agency, and between 1991 and 1994 was commissioned by London Northern, London United and Leaside Buses, all part of London Buses Ltd. Page 96.

JAMES H DOWD 1884–1956
He was primarily a draughtsman, etcher and painter who specialised in illustrations of children, particularly for books by Brenda Spender. From 1906 he contributed to *Punch*, and became the magazine's first film cartoonist.
5 posters, 1924–6. Page 37.

JEAN DUPAS 1882–1964
Born in Bordeaux, he studied at the Ecole Des Beaux Arts in Paris. In 1922 he won a gold medal at the Salon des Artistes Français, after which his decorative panels and poster designs became highly fashionable. Among several important commercial clients in France, Britain and the USA were the Sèvres porcelain factory and Saks department store in New York.
6 posters, 1930–3. Page 63.

TOM ECKERSLEY RDI b. 1914
Born in Lowton, Lancashire, he studied at Salford School of Art 1930–4. Together with his college friend Eric Lombers he moved to work in London, and in 1935 they were recommended by their former tutor to Frank Pick. They specialised in poster design and quickly gained a high reputation, producing work for many important clients including Shell, the General Post Office and the BBC. The partnership was brought to an end by the outbreak of the Second Word War, during which Eckersley worked as a cartographer in the RAF and produced a series of 'War Effort' posters. He was head of the Graphic Design Department at the London College of Printing from 1958 to 1977, and became a Royal Designer for Industry in 1963.
13 posters and 15 panel posters with Eric Lombers, 22 posters and 14 panel posters alone; 1935–95. Pages 66–67.

EDMUNDS
1 poster for London County Council Tramways, 1928. Page 43.

CLIFFORD ELLIS AND ROSEMARY ELLIS 1907–85 AND B. 1910
This husband-and-wife team worked together on poster designs for Shell, the Empire Marketing Board and the General Post Office, as well as London Transport. Between 1945 and 1982 they designed nearly 100 book jackets for the New Naturalist Series published by Collins. Clifford Ellis was Principal of Corsham Court, 1946–72.
12 posters and 9 panel posters, 1933–9. Pages 70 (below) and 76 (below).

FREDERICK WILLIAM CHARLES (JOHN) FARLEIGH 1900–65
In 1914 he became an articled apprentice to the Artists' Illustrators Agency and attended evening classes in drawing. From 1919 to 1922 he studied at the Central School of Arts and Crafts in London, where he was taught wood engraving by Noel Rooke. He then became an art instructor at Rugby School before returning, in 1925, to the Central School to teach. He was elected to the Society of Wood Engravers in 1925. His early posters for LCC Tramways were all signed F W Farleigh, but by 1933, when he designed his first poster for London Transport, he was already using the name John Farleigh. He is known particularly for his wood engravings, but also designed murals, stamps and posters, including one for the Post

Office. He painted in watercolours and pastels and exhibited widely. In 1947 he became Head of Book Production at the Central School, and in 1948 was elected a Fellow of the Royal Society of Painter-Etchers and Engravers. In the same year two of his posters for London Transport's Green Line coach services won awards from the International Poster Exhibition in Vienna. He was chairman of the Crafts Centre from 1950 to 1964. 20 posters for London Transport, 1922–63. Pages 34 (right) and 35.

VICTOR GALBRAITH

This artist emigrated to Australia in May 1966.
18 posters and 8 panel posters, 1957–66. Page 87.

ABRAM GAMES RDI b. 1914

Born in London, the son of an artist-photographer, Games attended art school for just six months, although he continued with evening classes while working for a commercial studio between 1932 and 1936. In 1935 he came first in a London County Council poster competition, after which he worked as a freelance poster artist from 1936 to 1940. During the Second World War he was appointed Official War Office Poster Designer, later assisted by Frank Newbould who also designed posters for London Transport. Following the war he specialised in designing posters and symbols, including the Festival of Britain and BBC TV symbols. He was a visiting lecturer in graphic design at the Royal College of Art 1946–53, and was made a Royal Designer for Industry in 1959.
18 posters and 1 panel poster, 1937–76. Page 89.

CLIVE GARDINER 1891-1960

Born in Blackburn, Lancashire, he studied first at the Slade School of Fine Art, 1909–12, and then the Royal Academy Schools, 1913–14. He taught art at Goldsmith's College of Art, and became its Principal in 1952.
27 posters, 1926–51. Pages 46 (right) and 47.

GWYNEDD M HUDSON FL. 1910–35

After studying at Brighton School of Art she specialised as a figure painter, poster artist and illustrator. Among the books she illustrated are editions of *Alice's Adventures in Wonderland* and *Peter Pan*.
2 posters, 1926–9. Page 40.

M JACKSON

1 poster, 1922. Page 24.

ARNRID BANNIZA JOHNSTON
b. 1895

Born in Uddevalla, Sweden, she came to London to study at the Slade School of Art. As well as a poster artist she was also a stone, marble and wood carver and a bronze and lead modeller. She exhibited at the Goupil, as well as the Whitechapel and other galleries.
8 posters and 3 panel posters, 1930–35. Pages 54, 56–57 and 60 (right).

RICHARD BARRETT TALBOT
KELLY RI 1896–1971

Son of the artist Robert George Talbot Kelly, he was educated first at Rugby School and then the Royal Military Academy, Woolwich. In 1917 he was wounded whilst serving in the Royal Artillery and became a camouflage instructor. A painter of birds in watercolour, he exhibited at the Royal Academy and Royal Institute of Painters in

Watercolours, to which he was elected in 1924, the Paris Salon and in the provinces. His published works include *The Way of Birds* (1937) and *Bird Life and the Painter*. He taught art at Rugby School. In 1951 he was design consultant for the Pavilion of Natural Science at the Festival of Britain. After his retirement in 1966 he illustrated books for the children's publisher Puffin.
3 posters, 1927–60. Page 46 (left).

R KNIGHT

1 poster, 1937. Page 75 (right).

FRANK MARSDEN LEA

4 posters for London County Council Tramways, 1928–32. Pages 58 (right) and 59.

BILL LEESON

He was a lino-cut artist.
2 posters, 1965–6. Page 86.

ERIC LOMBERS 1914–78

13 posters and 15 panel posters jointly with Tom Eckersley, 1935–9. Pages 66–67.

ENID CRYSTAL DOROTHY MARX
b. 1902

Born in London, she studied at the Central School of Arts and Crafts and the Royal College of Art. She was originally a designer of textiles with Barron and Larcher (1925–7) and later in her own studio. She also worked as a painter, printmaker and children's book illustrator, and as a designer of book jackets, trademarks and postage stamps. In 1937 Frank Pick commissioned designs for woollen moquette seating fabric for Underground trains from her. She was a member of the Design Panel of the Utility Furniture Advisory Committee (1944–7), the first

woman engraver to be appointed a Royal Designer for Industry (1944), and was elected a Fellow of the Society of Industrial Artists. She has taught and lectured on the history of textiles. With Margaret Lambert she published *English Popular and Traditional Art* in 1946 and *English Popular Art* in 1951.
3 posters, 1957–64. Pages 82 and 83.

MAURICE A MILES
In 1931 he exhibited at the Royal Academy. He designed a poster for Shell Mex and BP Ltd in 1933.
2 posters, 1934. Page 65.

UGO MOCHI
5 posters, 1922–3. Page 31 (above left).

M K MOUNTAIN
3 posters for London County Council Tramways, 1930–1. Pages 53 (above) and 56.

CHARLES PAINE
He studied at Salford College of Art and the Royal College of Art, then taught at Edinburgh College of Art. His poster designs for the Underground were mainly the result of his association with the Baynard Press, for whom he produced poster and other graphic designs for a large range of companies.
19 posters and 3 panel posters, 1920–9. Pages 26–27.

BIP PARES
He was a book illustrator and poster designer. His clients included Charles Clinkard in 1927.
2 posters, 1928–39. Page 77.

HERRY PERRY d. 1962
Heather (known as Herry) Perry studied at the London School of Arts and Crafts where she specialised in wood carving, though she later became a designer of posters, pub signs and playing cards. She contributed verse to *Punch*.
14 posters and 41 panel posters, 1927–37. Pages 45, 48 (left) and 61.

JOHN PLATT
1 poster, 1922. Page 29.

J MARTIN POLLOCK
1 poster, 1923. Page 30 (left).

MICHAEL REID
The first two posters of this photographer and designer won awards at the International Tourist Poster competition in Turin.
3 posters, 1968–76. Page 88.

REGINALD RIGBY
1 poster, 1915. Page 21.

WILLIAM ROBERTS 1895–1980
Born in Hackney, East London, he was the son of a carpenter. Roberts studied at St Martin's School of Art while apprenticed to an advertising firm. He attended the Slade School of Art in 1910–13, where he became interested in Cubism before joining the Vorticists in 1914. A painter in both oil and watercolours, he taught at the Central School of Arts and Crafts from 1925 to 1960, and exhibited at the Royal Academy from 1945 until his death. He was a war artist during both the First and Second World Wars. The Tate Gallery held a major retrospective exhibition of his work in 1965.
1 poster, 1 panel and 1 mural, 1953. Page 79.

ROJAN
1 poster, 1935. Page 70 (above).

MICHAEL ROSS
1 poster, 1936. Pages 72–73.

RUTH SANDYS
She designed a set of posters for the shoe firm of Lilley and Skinner Ltd between 1925 and 1930.
1 poster, 1925. Page 38.

EBERHARD SCHULZE
A mosaicist, he worked in conjunction with Hans Unger.
3 posters, 1962–70. Pages 84 and 85.

SENOTA
1 poster, 1915. Page 22 (left).

SHAFIG SHAWKI b. 1923
Born in Omdurman, Sudan, he graduated from Gordon Memorial College in Khartoum and then went on to receive a Sudan government scholarship to study and train as an art teacher. In 1945 he joined Goldsmith's College in London, where he studied under Carel Weight, John Piper and Betty Swanwick, who was impressed with his African talent and also his temperament. He was at Goldsmith's when he produced his only poster for London Zoo. In 1948 he returned to the Sudan to become the first Sudanese member of staff at the School of Design, Gordon College, later the Art Department of Khartoum Technical Institute.
1 poster, 1948. Page 78.

GEORGE SHERINGHAM 1884–1937
He studied art at the Slade School 1899–1901 and in Paris 1904–6, exhibiting in both Paris and

London. He was a book illustrator, poster artist and theatrical designer who also painted still-life subjects and landscapes.
5 posters, 1924–6. Page 36.

SMALL
1 poster, 1928. Pages 48 (right) and 49.

HAROLD STABLER 1872–1945
In addition to designing posters he was also an enameller, jeweller, silversmith, ceramic sculptor and potter. He was an instructor at the Royal College of Art and later Head of the Art Department at the Sir John Cass Technical Institute. He exhibited widely at the Royal Academy and elsewhere. His work is in several collections including the Victoria and Albert Museum and the Louvre, Paris. He produced many designs for Poole Pottery, where he was a director.
26 posters (including variations in the coronation series), 3 panel posters and 10 earthenware decorative tiles, 1923–37. Page 50 (below).

BETTY (ADA ELIZABETH EDITH) SWANWICK RA RWS 1915–89
Born in London, the daughter of a marine artist, she studied at Goldsmith's College of Art under Clive Gardiner and Edward Bawden, the Royal College of Art, and the Central School of Arts and Crafts. She was a tutor at Goldsmith's College 1948–69, a book illustrator, painter, designer and muralist.
9 posters and 2 panel posters, 1936–54. Page 80 (left).

HANS UNGER 1915–75
Born in Germany, he studied poster design in the Berlin studio of Jupp Wiertz in 1934–5. He then emigrated to South Africa to work as a freelance commercial designer in Cape Town. In 1948 he moved to London, where he became a successful poster designer. His posters include collaborations with the mosaicist Eberhard Schulze.
38 posters and 20 panel posters alone, 1950–74. Page 81.
4 posters with Eberhard Schulze, 1962–70. Pages 84 and 85.

VAN JONES
In 1941 he designed a poster of Berwick-upon-Tweed for the London and North Eastern Railway.
2 posters for London County Council Tramways, 1926–7. Page 41 (right).

SYDNEY THOMAS COOPER (OR CHARLES) WEEKS 1878
Born in Blackheath, South London, he was educated at Roan School, Greenwich and studied art at Heatherley's. He was a commercial artist and a member of the London Sketch Club.
5 posters and 4 panel posters, 1911–13. Page 20.

RACHEL WIDDOWS b. 1964
She studied at Hastings College of Art and Technology, 1983–4, and West Surrey College of Art and Design, Farnham, 1984–7, followed by an MA in fine art at the Royal Academy, 1987–90. Since 1987 she has exhibited widely, and her work has featured in the *Artist Illustrator* magazine. In 1993 she was Artist in Residence at Beaumanor Hall and Fulhurst Community College.
1 poster, 1993. Page 90.

LAWSON WOOD 1878–1957
Born in London, he studied at the Slade School and at Heatherley's. He specialised in humorous and animal subjects, and contributed to many magazines in Britain and overseas.
2 posters for London County Council Tramways, 1932–3. Pages 60 (left) and 62 (left).

MARY I WRIGHT
2 posters for London County Council Tramways, 1924–5. Page 31 (right).

ZERO (HANS SCHLEGER) RDI 1898–1976
Born in Germany, he studied at the National School of Applied Art in Berlin during the early 1920s. In 1924 he moved to New York, where he worked as a freelance graphic designer and later as an art director for an advertising agency. In 1932 he opened his own studio in London, and during the 1930s he designed numerous posters. He believed strongly in the concept of 'corporate identity', and in 1935 he designed the bus stop symbols for London Transport. Other major commissions included the symbols for the Design Centre in the Haymarket, London and for the Edinburgh International Festival 1966 (replaced 1978), as well as the creation of a unified design policy for a number of British companies. He was made a Royal Designer for Industry in 1959.
31 posters and 12 panel posters, 1935–47. Page 74 (above).

OLEG ZINGER
3 posters, 1933–7. Pages 62 (right) and 71.

For A Great Day Out at London Zoo
Terry Christien (Creative Design)
1993
8.5 × 4in/21 × 10cm

This leaflet issued by London Northern, then a subsidiary of London Buses, promotes a special service from the Zoo which is mainly operated by open-top buses.

Barman, Christian *The Man Who Built London Transport, A Biography of Frank Pick*, David and Charles 1979

The Buildings of London Zoo The Royal Commission on the Historial Monuments of England

Chalmers-Mitchell, P *The Zoological Society of London: Centenary History*, The Zoological Society of London 1929

Cole, Beverley and Richard Durack, *Railway Posters 1923–1947*, Laurence King 1992

Daily Occurrences, 1828–1970 The Zoological Society of London

Green, Oliver *Underground Art*, Studio Vista 1990

Green, Oliver and Jeremy Rowse-Davies *Design for London*, Laurence King 1995

Horne, Alan *The Dictionary of 20th Century Book Illustrators*, Antique Collectors' Club 1994

Hutchison, Harold F *London Transport Posters*, London Transport Board 1963

Huxley, Elspeth *Whipsnade*, Collins 1981

Jolly, WP *Jumbo*, Constable 1976

Keeling, Clinton *They All Came into the Ark*, Clam Publications 1988

Laver, James and Harold F Hutchison *Art for All*, Art and Technics 1949

Levy, Michael *London Transport Posters*, Phaidon/London Transport 1976

Riddell, Jonathan and William T Stearn *By Underground to Kew*, Studio Vista 1994

Scherren, Henry *The Zoological Society of London: A Sketch of Its Foundation and Development*, Cassell 1905

White, Charles *The Zoo*, Underground Railways 1915

The Zoological Society of London Annual Reports

1826–1976 and Beyond: Symposia, The Zoological Society of London 1976